DESIGN WITH SCRAP

Design with Scrap

CHRIS HOGGETT

ADAM & CHARLES BLACK · LONDON

First published 1980
by A & C Black (Publishers) Limited
35 Bedford Row, London WC1R 4JH

Text, drawings and photographs
© Chris Hoggett 1980
ISBN 0 7136 1723 3

British Library Cataloguing in Publication Data

Hoggett, Chris
   Design with scrap.
   1. Handicraft 2. Waste products
   I. Title
   745.5   TT880
    ISBN 0-7136-1723-3

Filmset and printed in Great Britain
by BAS Printers Limited, Over Wallop, Hampshire

Contents

**Each section has a detailed list of contents
on the first page.**

Acknowledgements

My grateful thanks are due to all those who have assisted me in the preparation of this book:

Barbara Alcock for her invaluable help with text, patterns and photographs on pages 162, 165, 166, 168–175 and 177–179 in the section on miscellaneous scrap.

Diana Anderson and Nancy Abbott for photographs on page 163.

Jane Levan for information on making the rubber costume accessories on pages 186–187.

Peter Etheredge for his animated paper prints on pages 56 and 57.

Surinder Ghalley for photographs and information on her collages with shells and other scrap material on pages 188 and 189.

Alex O'Sullivan for his paper sculpture figures on page 48.

Margaret Haynes for her group projects with primary school children using paper and card on pages 62 and 63.

John Wright for examples of layered wood-turning on page 29.

The children of Mitton Manor Primary School, Tewkesbury, Glos., of Wootton Wawen Primary School, Warks., of St. Joseph's Comprehensive School, Swindon, Wilts. and of Whitefriars School, Cheltenham, Glos. for the various art and craft examples illustrated in this book.

All the many people, shops, factories and companies who have so generously over the years provided me with loads of rubbish (scrap!)

My wife for her help and support during the preparation of this book.

C.H., Cheltenham

Introduction

This book is intended for all those who work on a slender budget or who welcome the challenge of designing with scrap materials. All the ideas in this book were developed from scrap and are pegs on which to hang a hundred more ideas.

Everything illustrated has been made from materials found, given or, in the case of some metal scrap, purchased at scrap prices. It takes a long time to discover or accumulate all the materials shown here and, of course, certain kinds of scrap not shown here will be available in some areas. Much will depend on the waste products of local industries.

It is easy to overlook the ordinary domestic rubbish discarded each week as its appearance is associated with the original function, e.g. as a food or drink container. If we look afresh at the commonplace scrap object, disregarding its original purpose and considering only its form, colour and texture, we may begin to see it as a source material for design.

The more unusual or strange scrap forms found among industrial or commercial waste may present an even greater challenge to the designer – the very strangeness and complexity of many pre-formed objects can be the spur for a wide range of craft projects. Many designers and craftsmen have a mental block about altering pre-designed or pre-formed objects (a large proportion of the scrap shown in this book) simply because the objects look resistant to change. This problem may be solved if the objects are altered or broken down into smaller units before being remade into something new.

As one example: the rigid expanded polystyrene packing case designed solely for the storage in transit of motorcycle parts (page 135). A study of this pre-formed object may suggest modifications which would allow the development of new forms. Expanded polystyrene sliced to half the thickness can suggest some kind of 'pierced wall' structure; cut into smaller parts, sawn and sanded, it can be used for various small individual sculptures; added to similar packing units, it can form a free-standing sculpture.

Technical explanation has been kept to a minimum as this book is planned to give visual information that will encourage readers to produce their own ideas and to develop their own techniques for expressing them.

Chisels and gouges

This book is not concerned with tools and their maintenance. However, a brief reference to chisels and gouges is pertinent to any sections that deal with carving techniques. Carving tools differ from woodworking tools in that both sides of the cutting edge have to be honed (sharpened). For those wishing to develop carving, a full detailed study of honing techniques is recommended. (A good technical handbook is *Woodcarving for Beginners* by Charles Graveney, Studio Vista.)

Choice of chisels and gouges

These tools are classified by *shape* (straight, curved or bent), by *width* (at the cutting edge) and by *section* (shape at the cutting edge).

Only 5 tools of the straight shape are needed by a beginner – the $\frac{1}{2}$ in (13 mm) width is the most useful.
a flat chisel (no. 1)
a skew chisel – 45° edge (no. 2)
three gouges (nos. 4, 6 and 9)

For the more experienced straight gouges nos. 1. 2 and 7 are useful – also a small 'V' gouge.

The stones

The most practical type is the combination stone with medium and fine grain on opposite sides. A natural stone called Washita is used for honing to a near razor-sharp finish. Small curved slipstones are used to hone the inside of gouges.

combination stone   Washita stone   slip stones

Sharpening a chisel

First secure the stone in a home-made box to prevent it slipping and lightly lubricate the stone with a thin oil. Sharpen the chisel flat on the bevel at an angle of approximately 15° as shown in illustration top right.

Push forwards firmly, checking that you keep an even bevel. You will find a fine burr of metal on the edge – turn the chisel over and hone the burr away.

Repeat the process using the fine grain side of the stone. This will usually be adequate for school use. For a finer razor-sharp edge, use the Washita stone and then strop on leather.

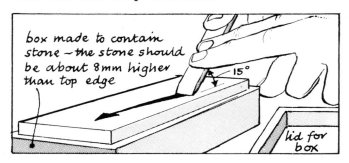

box made to contain stone – the stone should be about 8mm higher than top edge

15°

lid for box

Sharpening a gouge

The outer bevel is first sharpened on the medium grain side of the stone. Sharpen the gouge as shown, using a swinging motion across the curved edge, the hand rotating.

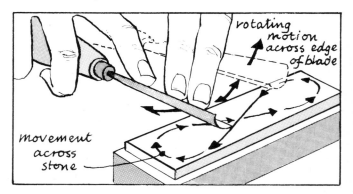

rotating motion across edge of blade

movement across stone

Repeat the process with finer stones, as for the chisel. Then hone the inside bevel with an appropriate slipstone to fit the curvature of the gouge. Only a slight bevel need be developed on the inside. Push the slipstone gently across at the 15° angle until any burr is removed.

Wood

1

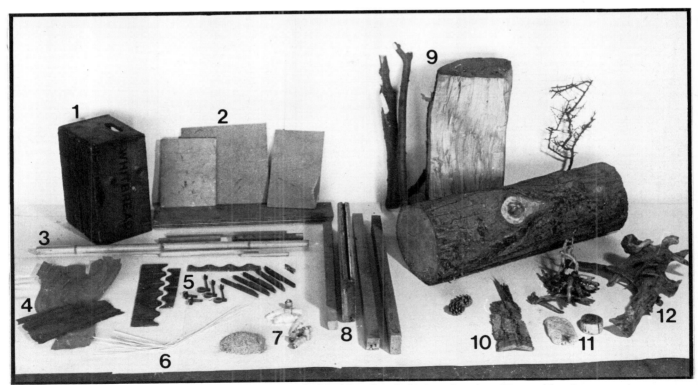

1 wooden boxes and crates; 2 boards, laminated plywoods, blockboard and chipboard; 3 dowelling and bamboos; 4 veneers; 5 pre-formed pieces (for piano see Miscellaneous Scrap section); 6 cane; 7 wooden debris, sawdust and shavings; 8 wood strip and batten; 9 tree trunk, branch and twig; 10 bark; 11 cork; 12 roots

SCRAP WOOD

Scrap wood can be divided into two groups: natural forms and man-made forms.

Natural forms include the trunk, branches, twigs, roots and bark of a tree, all of which can be carved.

Man-made forms include all laminated boards (plywoods and blockboards), chipboards and veneers; wood shavings, chippings and sawdust; pre-formed and machined pieces (e.g. piano keys and action); and offcuts.

Sources of supply
Sources for each item are included under each page heading.

Storage
Store small pieces of wood (blocks and plywood offcuts) in boxes and tea chests, stacked one on top of the other. If wall space is available, it is worthwhile constructing a deep rack of shelving to store sawn branches, logs and bark, with smaller items at the top.

Tools
Only a few essential tools are required but they should be of the best quality steel. A few tools not illustrated here are useful time-savers: the electric jig and band saws have an obvious advantage in cutting out irregular shapes.

The method of sharpening chisels and gouges can be found on page viii.

Tools

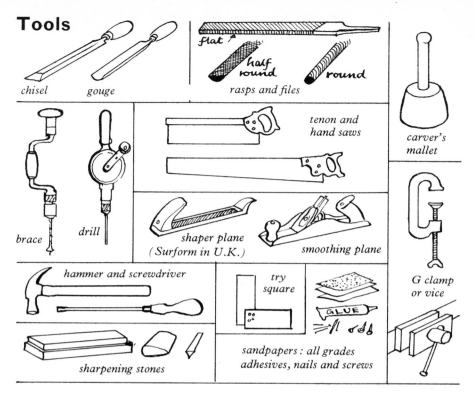

chisel   gouge   flat
                          half round   round
                          rasps and files

brace   drill

                    tenon and hand saws

shaper plane (Surform in U.K.)   smoothing plane

hammer and screwdriver

try square

GLUE

sandpapers: all grades
adhesives, nails and screws

sharpening stones

carver's mallet

G clamp or vice

WOOD BLOCK – 1
Touch forms

The block
Workshops and building sites dispose of large quantities of softwood blocks. Timber yards and sawmills usually have oddments that can be cut to shorter block length at home. Ensure that all wood is dry before use.

Select a piece of softwood sufficient in length and width to accommodate your idea and add an extra 10 cm to the length for clamping to the bench – this will allow free access to all parts of the block whilst carving.

Touch forms
Small hand-held forms are termed 'touch forms', shapes that can be handled with pleasure, especially by the young child.

Two or more such forms may be related to each other on a base board and held in place with screws from the underside. Here are the first steps towards free-standing sculpture.

Tools
You will need either a gouge or a chisel for roughing out the basic shape; a rasp or shaper plane/file for smoothing down and rounding off corners; a tenon or any small saw; sandpaper for the final polish and a G clamp or vice to hold the block to the bench.

Method

Before working on the block look at a few natural forms – pebbles collected from the seashore or shells, worn pieces of wood, fruits and trees. A few quick sketches may suggest shapes for the block, or you may see a suitable form without sketching anything – or the grain pattern is sometimes so clearly defined in a block of wood that the form can be 'seen' within it.

However you do it, you must have a rough idea of the shape you are aiming at: convex overall or concave on one side; long and narrow, or squat; pear-shaped or twisting.

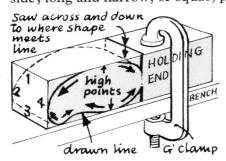

1 Choose a shape that touches the four sides of the block. Outline the shape on one side. Arrows show which way to cut with the grain of wood by working from high to low points. A saw cut must be made between the shape and the holding end, down to where the shape outline is drawn.

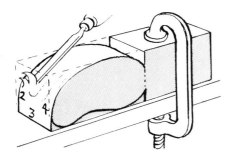

2 Rough out side 1 with the gouge or chisel at an angle of 15° to the working surface. Then use the shaper plane or rasp to smooth down the surface. Repeat on side 3.

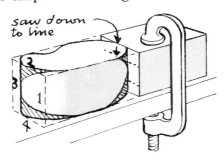

3 Sketch your shape on one of the curved sides and turn the block onto side 2. Now carve out the shaded areas. Turn your block to side 4 and repeat the process. Saw down to your shape as in 1.

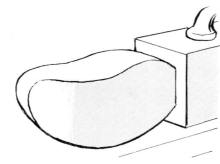

4 When the four sides have been carved and smoothed to the desired curves, four curved 'edges' will remain. These can be smoothed down or not as you decide. A contrast of hard and soft 'edges' can be interesting – or you may decide to make the whole form as smooth as a pebble.

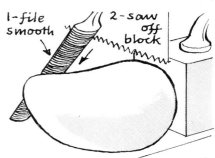

5 The final smoothing down with rasp or shaper file and plane. Finally saw the touch form from the holding piece. This will leave one end to be rounded off and smoothed.

Finish the smoothing with medium and fine sandpaper. Coat the form once or twice with varnish – or furniture polish for a semi-gloss. Wood stain may be used to colour the wood.

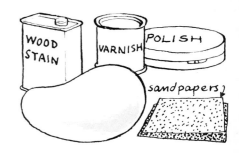

Some examples of touch forms in soft woods by 12 year olds are shown on page 5.

3

2 Free-standing forms

Long offcuts from block or batten can be used for first attempts at free-standing sculpture. (They can be attached to a base.) Forms can be naturalistic or abstract. They will help the beginner to acquire practice in the use of certain basic tools: the square, tenon saw, chisel and mallet, gouge, brace and bit, file/rasp and shaper plane.

The following sequence of illustrations shows the development of a simple form with a vertical/horizontal emphasis in the design.

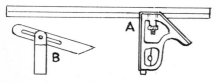

1 Marking-out with a try square. Hold the metal stock firmly against the top of the block and mark lines across as required. For angles use a combination (A) or sliding bevel (B) square.

2 Sawing along the marked lines to the depth required. The saw could also be used to cut out angled or wedge-shaped pieces.

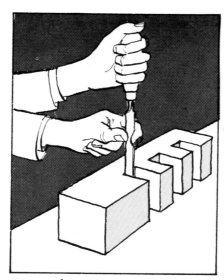

3 Removing the sawn pieces with a chisel and paring off (or cleaning out) the space. A mallet may be used with the chisel to remove the sawn pieces before paring if the wood is hard.

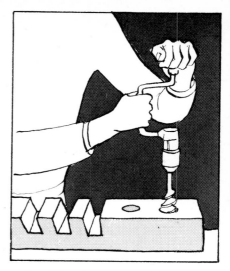

4 Drilling holes with a brace and bit. Try all kinds of shapes including some with holes and hollows. In this case holes are being drilled into and through the block.

5 Opening out a drilled hole with a gouge. This shows the correct holding method for carving with a gouge. All carved parts of the block form can be rounded out with the gouge and then with the shaper plane or rasp. Finally sandpaper smooth and varnish.

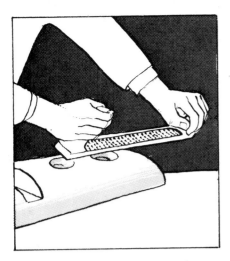

6 Using the Surform or shaper plane to curve and then to smooth the curved surface.

Touch forms in soft woods by 12 year olds. Method described on page 3.

Variations on the free-standing form in 75 × 75 mm square wood block. Carving by 13 year olds.

WOOD STRIP

Perhaps the most plentiful of all scrap woods, wood strip can be found fairly easily. Ask at building sites, timber yards, builders' merchants, furniture manufacturers, etc. Very often the strips are in perfect condition for making strip constructions like those below. Wood strip is a useful material for all forms of linear structure in three-dimensional projects, stimulating the spatial sense of design work in architectural and theatre forms.

If a large quantity of strips of one particular width and thickness is required use a circular saw bench.

It is not necessary to purchase a specific adhesive for this or many of the projects in this book – many alternatives are acceptable for lightweight interior woodwork. PVA, casein glues and traditional animal (Scotch) glues are all suitable.

Larger, heavier strips can be pinned after gluing with panel pins or small oval nails.

Strips can be left as natural wood, or can be stained or painted. Plastic emulsion paint is particularly suitable for structures of this kind.

Below : wood strips combined with acrylic offcuts (see pages 156–7)

 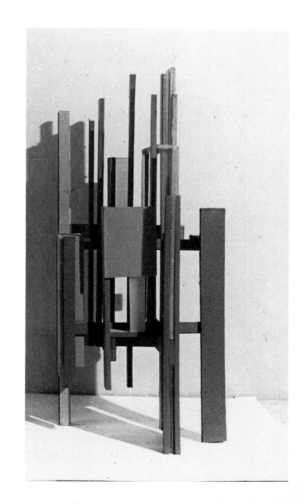

LOGS – 1: Twigs and branches

The natural tendency to whittle wood (to cut wood back with a penknife) can be developed into a strong craft form if larger twigs or thin branches are substituted – particularly thin branches with one or more offshoots.

A child will often carve out the 'hidden' form if encouraged to discover something within the wood.

Essential tools are a flat gouge or chisel, a file or Surform shaper plane, and some sandpaper for smoothing (Garnet paper lasts longer). A G-clamp or vice will be needed to hold the wood that is being carved.

Holding and carving

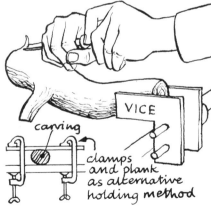

Secure the wood in a clamp or vice and hold the gouge or chisel firmly in both hands – one gripping the handle to push forward, the other holding the shaft both to guide and control the forward thrust (thus acting as a brake to prevent the cutting edge from going too far).

Three willow branch forms by 13 year olds: the creature on the left could have forearms added by having two holes drilled and smaller twigs inserted. The slug-like creature in the foreground could have a shell of carved wood added. The standing figure is being sanded smooth and will later be attached to a base.

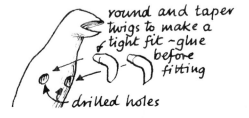

Small twigs can be shaped and fitted into drilled holes for any additional features or 'missing limbs'. Here are the forearms to fit the left-hand form in the picture above.

LOGS – 2: Tree trunks and branches

Branches and trunks from a felled tree can be found in timber yards, farmyards, woodpiles and much open country. Look especially in woodland, copses, etc. for fallen branches. Try tree-felling specialists for advice and availability of timber.

Unlike the wood block which is shaped by saw and plane, the natural plant forms offer more scope for creative wood design. Most wood can be carved, shaped and sawn although it is advisable to use only softwood for beginners and the younger child. This includes cedar, fir, pine, willow and lime. The more experienced carver can use oak, apple, elm, beech and other hardwood.

The next few pages show three-dimensional woodcraft from the small branch to large sections of tree trunk. All examples are worked from waste pieces of tree.

Found forms

Encouragement to look closely and seek out a 'hidden form' within the twist and turn of a branch can often be, for many beginners in woodcraft, the starting point for many creative and imaginative three-dimensional ideas.

Young children and all beginners in carving will usually respond to the shape of twigs and branches with offshoots far more readily than to a block of wood. Their interest in the craft will be more genuine.

1 A section of branch with two offshoots from one side. Explore its form from all angles. Do the two shoots suggest limbs, horns, arms or something else?

3 After removing the bark, sketch out a side view with felt-tip or chalk. Saw and carve away outside the shape.

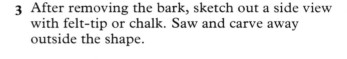

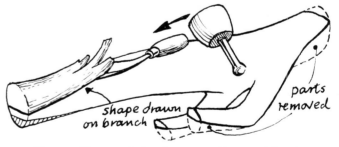

shape drawn on branch

parts removed

2 For the form 'seen' within the branch the shaded parts would have to be sawn and carved away. But first the bark must be removed with a gouge or chisel.

4 Carve all round the form until your idea is sufficiently developed. Then file and sandpaper the surface to a smooth finish. Prepare a base, ensuring that the form stands level with it, and secure with screws.

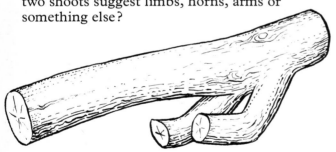

outline drawn with fibre tip pen

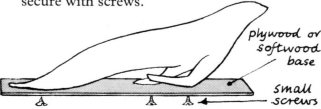

plywood or softwood base

small screws

8

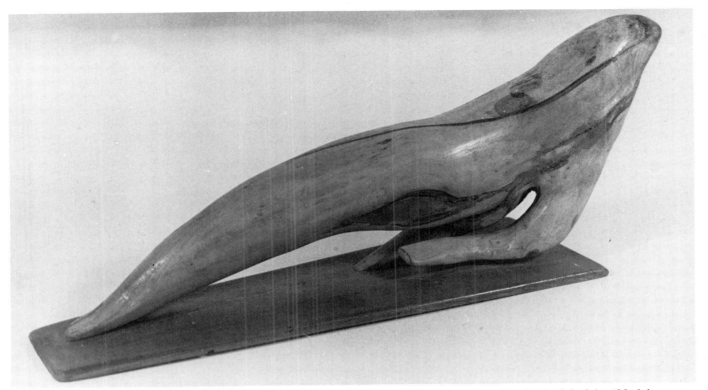

The finished carving: a seal in pine on a thin ply base. It is coated with varnish, but it could also be waxed, stained or left plain. (Made by 15 year old.)

The sketch on the right shows another way of using the same piece of wood: the head of a deer mounted on a wall plate.

The branch has been shortened by sawing. The flippers of the seal shown above have become the horns of the deer by a slight modification of the shape. Eyes are carved, nostrils drilled and mouth sawn out. Finally the carving is secured to a wall plate.

By turning this and similar pieces of wood in the hand and covering up parts with a piece of card, you may think of other ideas to develop from this same branch!

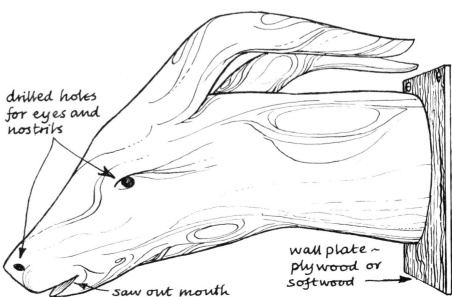

drilled holes for eyes and nostrils

saw out mouth

wall plate – plywood or softwood

LOGS – 3: Split pieces of log

Large logs and complete sections of sawn tree trunks often have wide cracks running down the length of the wood. These cracks can be used to split apart the wood with an axe or with wedges and a mallet. This will produce a wide variety of pieces for carving.

A trunk section similar to the one which provided all the pieces used for making the forms shown on the opposite page.

Standing forms

Try developing the touch forms shown on page 3 with larger pieces of wood.

Suitable preparation for this kind of carving includes studies of bone structures, plants and sea creatures. Draw sketches to the scale of the wood – and sketch the outlines on the wood itself to assist in the cutting-out.

Carving and drilling holes

Holes through pieces of carving can add another dimension to comparatively flat work, giving windows to other forms lying beyond. After drilling a wide hole, try extending and thinning the edge but only on one side and at the top. Turn the work round and carve only at the bottom edge.

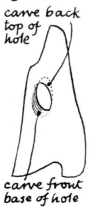

carve back top of hole

carve front base of hole

Illustrated opposite is a group of forms based on animal bone structures by fourth-year examination students of three-dimensional design. All the pieces were taken from one log split down with an axe. The central pieces were stained before the final coats of varnish and wax were applied.

All the forms were carved with gouges 4 and 9.

Figure against standing form. This carving uses two pieces of lime offcuts fixed to a redwood base. (Made by 14 year old.)

Front view showing ears, drilled nostrils and sawn-out mouth.

Right and top right, a fine example of the offshoot branches of a large log being used as four legs. The pig's ears were cut from the same piece of branch and set into a sawn groove at a suitable angle – and then undercut. The tail was carved out carefully to avoid splitting the open grain of the pine log. The remains of the cambium layer just under the bark can be seen on the underside of the pig. This gives an attractive patterning to the surface. (Work of 13 year old.)

saw and carve off excess branches

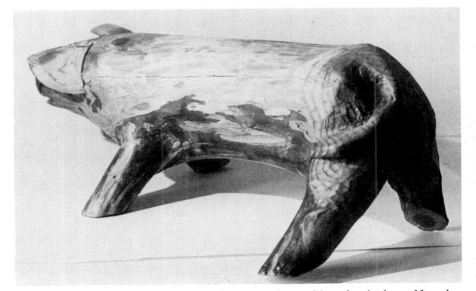

This is the actual shape of the log before it is cut and carved into the pig shape. Note that occasionally limbs have to be removed rather than added.

It was looking 'within' the wood (see page 8) that suggested the carving of this pig form.

LOGS – 4: Tree trunks

Complete sections of tree trunk can be carved with large gouges into sculpture-in-the-round. Large heads and animals are within the scope of young hands – the forms illustrated here were carved by 13 to 15 year olds.

Left : the scream. A hole in the trunk was used for a mouth. Scotch pine.

Black rhinoceros : first cut out with a saw and chisel, then carve with gouges and smooth with a file. Stained pine.

Four heads, carved in Scotch pine, mahogany, oak and pine.

All the examples below were carved from complete sections of lime trunk or log. They could equally well have been worked in other woods. It is important, especially in schools or colleges, to utilise any kind of scrap wood. Most is suitable for carving – wood recently felled can be stored in a garage or shed to be seasoned for a few months. If sawn ends are painted before storage, this will prevent wood drying out too quickly at the ends – a common cause of cracks.

Tools
For information about the sharpening of tools, refer to notes on page viii or to books on wood crafts.

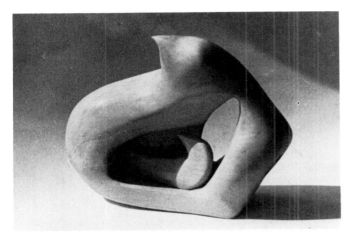

Form within a form – a large carving in lime with a small form set within it.

Below : the wrestlers. This pair of figures was carved from a large section of trunk.

Turning form, based on bone studies.

BARK – 1

Bark can be found on fallen or dead trees and branches – or on branches that have been pruned from a tree or shrub. Look, especially in stormy weather, for any fallen timber and enquire of the owner if you may remove bark or whole branches. Local tree-felling companies and tree surgeons may be able to advise and, in some cases, to provide bark.

Store different kinds of bark in a large box until you have collected enough for your particular purposes.

Warning
On no account strip bark from a standing tree unless the tree is completely dead and you have the owner's permission. Such stripping will do irreparable damage to the tree and is quite unnecessary. Rather, look for loose pieces of fallen bark in parks, gardens and the countryside – and ask around when pruning is taking place.

Bark on the branch
Bark can be left on parts of a carving to represent fur, hide or any other rough texture.

Head of an imaginary beast: the face is stripped and the bark behind the face left on to represent fur or hide. (Carved by a 12 year old.)

Stripping bark from trunk or branch
Large pieces of bark can be prised free from the trunk or branch provided that there are enough wedges to hold bark and wood apart during the operation.

Start with a wide iron wedge, axe head or wide chisel and then proceed as below.

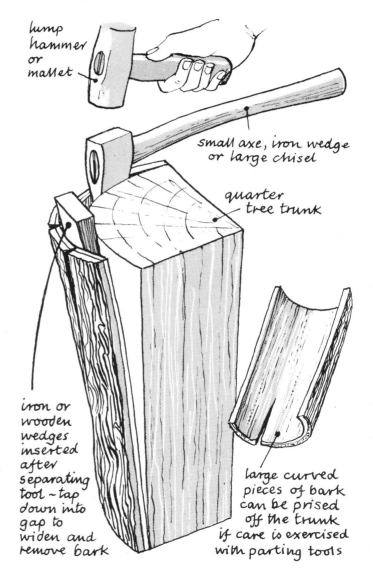

lump hammer or mallet

small axe, iron wedge or large chisel

quarter tree trunk

iron or wooden wedges inserted after separating tool – tap down into gap to widen and remove bark

large curved pieces of bark can be prised off the trunk if care is exercised with parting tools

14

Porcupine

This small porcupine has spines cut from the cambium (inner layer of bark) from a lime tree. Body and feet were carved from a branch and twigs of a Scotch pine. Note how the spines become thinner and smaller towards the head.

Drive a wide chisel deep between bark and cambium layer. Insert another chisel or metal bar in the opening alongside the chisel. Pull tools in opposite directions prising the layers apart. Repeat as necessary and then reverse in the vice and proceed from the other end.

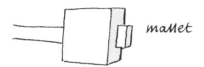

mallet

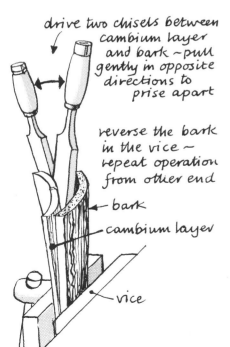

drive two chisels between cambium layer and bark ~ pull gently in opposite directions to prise apart

reverse the bark in the vice ~ repeat operation from other end

bark

cambium layer

vice

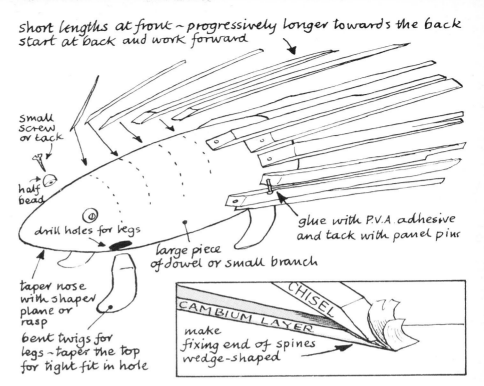

short lengths at front ~ progressively longer towards the back start at back and work forward

small screw or tack

half bead

drill holes for legs

taper nose with shaper plane or rasp

bent twigs for legs ~ taper the top for tight fit in hole

large piece of dowel or small branch

glue with P.V.A. adhesive and tack with panel pins

CHISEL

CAMBIUM LAYER

make fixing end of spines wedge-shaped

Porcupine by 13 year old: the construction is shown at the top of the page. Other creatures such as the hedgehog and armadillo could be constructed in a similar way.

BARK – 2: Sculpture

Larger projects using bark need a strong supporting framework. This will have to be constructed first. The large eagle shown here is 1·5 metres high with a wing span of 2 metres, and is secured to a baseboard with PVA adhesive and screws.

Take a 25 mm thick piece of blockboard or chipboard and attach to it (by screwing from the underside of the board) a suitable piece of branch for the bird to perch on.

Select pieces of wood for the frame:

Body 50 mm thick plank
Neck 50 × 50 mm softwood
Head a touch form (see below)
Wings 25 × 75 mm and 25 × 50 mm for lower and upper wings
Legs two pieces of hardboard; dowelling
Talons suitable large twigs with plenty of twists and turns. The example illustrated has apple wood talons.

Head

glued and tacked bark

bead →

TOUCH FORM

shaded areas removed with fret or coping saw

For making touch forms, see page 3.

Eagle: base of 25 mm plywood; log of Scotch pine; talons of apple wood; feathers of lime bark; head of pine; supporting framework of assorted softwood scrap pieces.

Construction for eagle

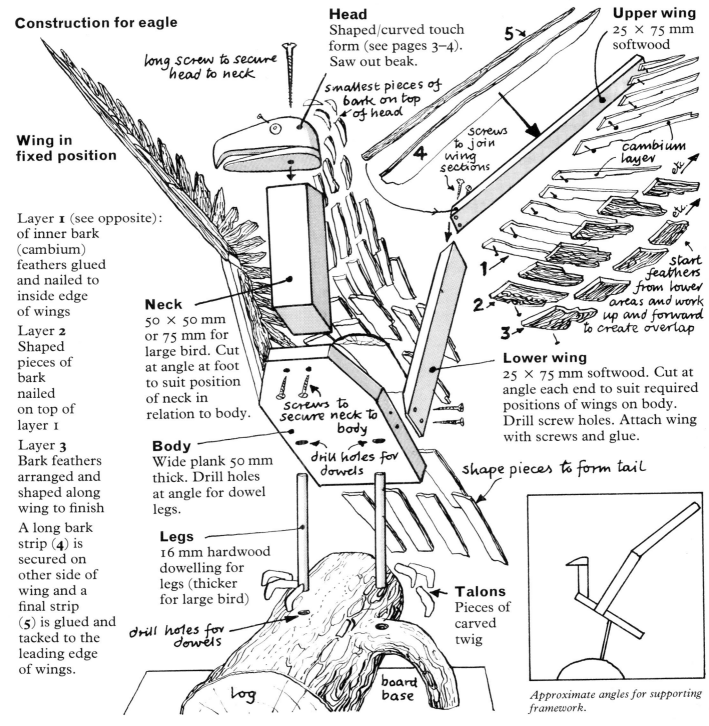

long screw to secure head to neck

Wing in fixed position

Head
Shaped/curved touch form (see pages 3–4). Saw out beak.

smallest pieces of bark on top of head

Upper wing
25 × 75 mm softwood

5

4

screws to join wing sections

cambium layer

etc

etc

start feathers from lower areas and work up and forward to create overlap

1

2

3

Layer **1** (see opposite): of inner bark (cambium) feathers glued and nailed to inside edge of wings

Layer **2** Shaped pieces of bark nailed on top of layer **1**

Layer **3** Bark feathers arranged and shaped along wing to finish

A long bark strip (**4**) is secured on other side of wing and a final strip (**5**) is glued and tacked to the leading edge of wings.

Neck
50 × 50 mm or 75 mm for large bird. Cut at angle at foot to suit position of neck in relation to body.

Body
Wide plank 50 mm thick. Drill holes at angle for dowel legs.

screws to secure neck to body

drill holes for dowels

Lower wing
25 × 75 mm softwood. Cut at angle each end to suit required positions of wings on body. Drill screw holes. Attach wing with screws and glue.

shape pieces to form tail

Legs
16 mm hardwood dowelling for legs (thicker for large bird)

drill holes for dowels

log

board base

Talons
Pieces of carved twig

Approximate angles for supporting framework.

17

BARK – 3: Sculpture with metals

The owl illustrated here shows a combination of metal and bark. This combination offers some interesting possibilities for three-dimensional design: extremes of textural contrast between the bright, highly polished and smooth surfaces of the metals, and the very rough, matt and uneven texture of barks.

Experiments could include bark landscape with metal constructions hinting at industrial complexes ... or water reflections ...

The construction of the owl is shown on the right. A quarter round section of tree trunk is the base and the body is built up in the same way as that for the eagle on the previous page – but without any wings. Note the need to get a near-vertical stance to the owl's body. This requires that you drill at the correct angle for dowelling by marking the angle on the sides of the plank before drilling.

When adding the bark overlay, always begin at the tail and work upwards to the head; this will ensure the natural overlay of feathers.

Other suitable projects for bark sculpture

All feathered and spined creatures – large birds, porcupines, etc.; 'armour-plated' animals – rhinoceroses, armadillos and 'dragons'.

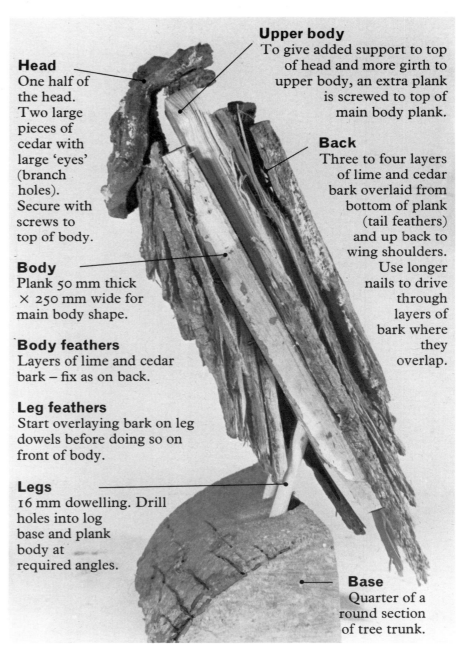

Head
One half of the head. Two large pieces of cedar with large 'eyes' (branch holes). Secure with screws to top of body.

Body
Plank 50 mm thick × 250 mm wide for main body shape.

Body feathers
Layers of lime and cedar bark – fix as on back.

Leg feathers
Start overlaying bark on leg dowels before doing so on front of body.

Legs
16 mm dowelling. Drill holes into log base and plank body at required angles.

Upper body
To give added support to top of head and more girth to upper body, an extra plank is screwed to top of main body plank.

Back
Three to four layers of lime and cedar bark overlaid from bottom of plank (tail feathers) and up back to wing shoulders. Use longer nails to drive through layers of bark where they overlap.

Base
Quarter of a round section of tree trunk.

The photograph shows the halfway stage of construction. It is important at this stage to check that all angles of the body are correct in relation to the base and that the girth of the body is not too great.

The completed owl: the legs could be covered in wood only, with twigs for the talons, as shown for the eagle. Finish the completed sculpture with a matt-finish polyurethane or oil varnish if bark has been used (unnecessary on rust-free metals).

Construction of eyes and beak

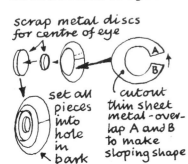

scrap metal discs for centre of eye

set all pieces into hole in bark

cutout thin sheet metal – overlap A and B to make sloping shape

tabs can be used to secure beak between eye pieces

shape from thin sheet metal – score and fold centre

Construction of feet

Use thin metal sheet: the thickness of an old lithographic plate is quite sufficient, although a more robust metal sheet could be used.

1 Cut out eight series of shapes for the number of joints required on all the talons. The largest and longest pieces have two tabs to be wrapped round the dowelling legs.

centre top

cut out dart shape – close gap to make claw

2 Wrap each shaped piece round a pencil or cylindrical object smaller than the required size. As metal tends to spring back, a smaller curve is easier to use. Each piece can be fixed with Evostik Impact adhesive or with wire. Provided that the metal is not aluminium, the fixing agent can be solder.

wrap each piece round pencil or any cylindrical object

3 Join the pieces in series as shown:

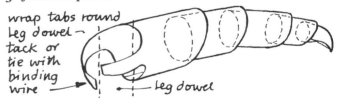

wrap tabs round leg dowel – tack or tie with binding wire

leg dowel

4 Make four talons for each foot, one to curve down behind the log.

5 Prepare carefully two arched pieces of metal for the visible parts of the legs. Each piece will have three arches to fit over the three front talons of each foot. The back of the leg is not easily seen, so the back talon can be fixed without a metal arch over it.

wrap round leg dowel →

PLANKING – 1: Relief carving

Offcuts from planking 100 mm or wider can often be found at building sites or at houses, offices and shops undergoing conversion. Occasionally small pieces of well-seasoned wood can be unearthed in a garden shed, attic or cellar. All such oddments can be used for relief work, unless they are of very hard wood. Lime, cedar and pine are all soft and easy to carve, and are the most suitable woods for beginners.

Two kinds of relief carving can be attempted. The design can be drawn on the wood, and the surrounding areas be carved away to leave about one third of the total thickness. Alternatively, the areas around the design shape can be cut away completely with a coping or bandsaw. This pierced, cut-out relief can then be set against a contrasting wood or against the light to create a silhouette effect.

A basic design

The beginner should choose a shape with a simple uncluttered outline, such as the natural form of some fish, leaves or birds. Complex shapes should be avoided until a carving technique has been developed.

1 Select a suitably dry and flat piece of planking, smooth it down with plane and/or sandpaper if necessary, and draw out a design.

2 Draw small rough sketches of the object you wish to carve.

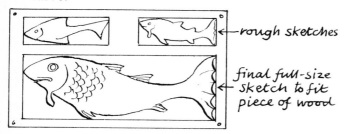

rough sketches

final full-size sketch to fit piece of wood

Draw round your piece of wood on a piece of paper to give the exact size. Then draw out your design to full scale. When you are satisfied with the design, transfer to the wood by drawing over your sketch through a piece of carbon paper on to the wood. Alternatively, you may prefer to draw straight onto the wood.

3 Once the shape is outlined on the wood itself, draw a line round the edge of the wood to indicate the level down to which you want to carve – half to two-thirds is the normal cutting depth.

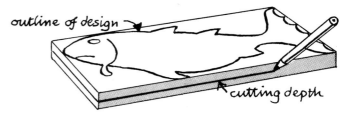

outline of design

cutting depth

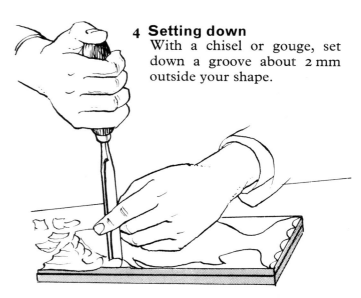

4 **Setting down**
With a chisel or gouge, set down a groove about 2 mm outside your shape.

5 **Cutting across**
Cut from the front edge of the wood horizontally as far as the 'setting down' outline.

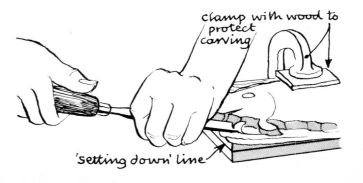

clamp with wood to protect carving

'setting down' line

The process of setting down and cutting across is continued until the required depth is reached (see **3**). No undercutting should be attempted at this stage. The shape should have vertical 'walls' cut down to 'ground' level. Level and smooth off the ground with a flat gouge or chisel.

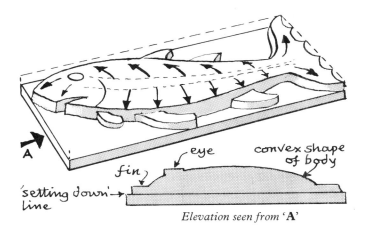

Elevation seen from 'A'

6 Shaping

Take down the level of the fins to half the height of the fish. The tail fin may remain high or low according to your choice of position. Start carving the body from centre spine area down the sides to make a *convex* shape. Carve round the eye carefully before removing any wood from the head. The eye will later be rounded off as a protruding shape. The arrows in the diagram above show the approximate directions for cutting.

7 Modelling and patterning

When the main form of the relief has been carved, more detailed features can be worked. Ensure that all sides of the main body have been taken down right to the background. At this stage undercutting can be attempted if desired. The tail may be left high with undercutting to suggest the thinness. The eye may be rounded out with a gouge which fits closely to the shape.

Scales Select a gouge with a deep curve (or use a 'V' gouge) and follow a pencil line for the first row of scales. On the second row, alternate the cuts so that points of curve just touch the rounded centres of the previous row. Continue alternating cuts until you reach rear of body. It is advisable to use a mallet to make any vertical cuts.

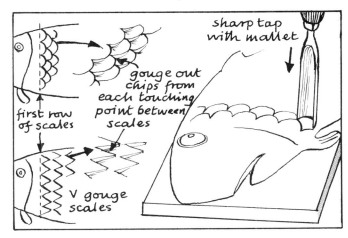

Note : Use a mallet for the setting-down stage (see **4**) if children are doing the carving. They would be unable to exert sufficient pressure or control by hand alone.

Examples of small relief fishes by 12 year olds (see previous page)

PLANKING – 2: Relief carving (continued)

The development from final sketch to finished work is shown here in a relief carving by a fourteen-year-old.

The top illustration shows the sketch – two skateboarders – marked out clearly on the wood. The left-hand side has been set down to the background and cut across into the base of the 'walls' – note the vertical plane of the wall. Note also the absence of a clamp where the work can be pushed against a stop – in this case a batten secured along the centre of the bench and clamped at each end.

As the work proceeded, the right-hand figure was taken to a lower level to represent a skateboarder in a more distant position. The finished work is shown in the lower photograph.

Right Three reliefs in lime wood, all by fifteen year olds: a hare, a hanging man and a heraldic device.

The lower illustration of a tortoise shows the use of stain to create a contrast of colour. Note the scaling on the legs, embossed with a small gouge, and the large hexagonal shapes on the shell cut out with a chisel. The centres of the hexagons remain high. (Made by 14 year old.)

PLANKING – 3: Chip carving

Offcuts suitable for relief carving may also be used for chip carving – one of the earliest forms of carving.

Design and pattern are largely determined by the tool used – the chisel or gouge. Wedge-shaped pockets are cut into the flat surface with the chisel, moon-shaped pockets with the gouge. All patterns are based on these two cuts.

Marking out

Take a softwood plank offcut about 20 mm thick and sand or plane it if necessary to give a smooth, flat surface.

Draw a set of parallel lines along the length of the grain, set apart by the width of the chisel (**A**). Divide across into squares, again using the chisel width (**B**).

Cutting (Stepping down)

'Stepping down' or cutting vertically into the line is shown on right. Hold the shaft of the chisel as shown and tap gently with a mallet to a depth of approximately 2 mm. Repeat this cut along the line of squares to the end, retaining the same cutting angle.

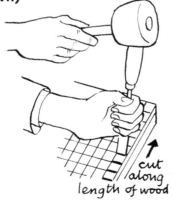

cut along length of wood

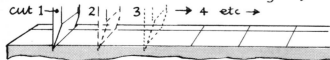

cut 1→ | 2 | 3 → 4 etc →

Note: If the wood is very soft, hand pressure alone will make the first cuts. Harder woods require the use of a mallet – young children will need a mallet even for soft woods.

Removing the chip

left hand (brake)

right hand (guide)

chip

The correct way to hold the chisel when removing the chip is shown above – note the low cutting angle. If the left-hand knuckle touches the surface of the wood, the angle will be approximately correct for the 2 mm vertical cut. Complete a row of chips in one direction, and then repeat the same operation in the opposite direction.

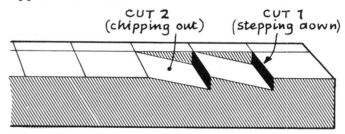

CUT 2 (chipping out)   CUT 1 (stepping down)

Cross-section alongside the first line of squares, showing the first two cuts.

The triangular chip

Another kind of chip cut is the triangle. The chisel is again set square to the drawn line, but with one corner lifted so that the cut is deeper at point **A**. A similar cut is made along the crossing line, again deeper at point **A**. A third cut removes the chip: the chisel is held parallel to the length of the plank and the cut made at a tilting angle to meet the first two cuts.

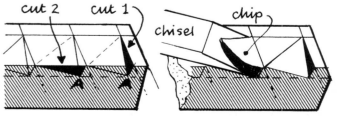

cut 2   cut 1   chip   chisel

Cross-sections showing angles of cutting the triangular chip.

Double triangle

A left-hand triangle meeting a right-hand triangle at a centre line will make a double triangle. When repeated along a complete line of squares this will create a moving zig-zag line. Many variations of this basic triangular pocket are possible. Experiment with cuts that differ in length, curve and position.

1 Triangle along the edge of plank.

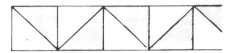

2 Basic cut across line.

3 Alternating triangles making zig-zags.

4 Alternating triangles with the first cuts angled inwards to give wing-shaped pockets, three-sided.

Chip carvings by fourteen-year-old children using Parana pine offcuts.

5 Reversing the second row of triangles to give lozenge shapes.

Gouge cut chip carving

Gouge cuts are made in a similar way, with first a vertical cut and then a horizontal chip cut. However, there is a difference: the chip cut must be made on the convex side of the first cut. And the first cut should be angled at about 10 degrees towards the second cut in order to ease the removal of the chip.

Variations of the basic moon-shaped cut:
a 1st cut close to 2nd; **b** 2nd cut at low angle; **c** 2nd cut further away – at even lower angle.

Alternating direction of moon in adjacent rows produces continuous wave motion.

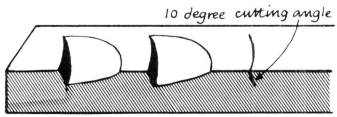

Cross-section of moon-shaped gouge cuts.

Scale patterns – gouge moves along half a square on succeeding rows. See examples of chip scaling on the fishes on page 21.

25

PLANKING – 4: Bowls, platters and servers

The shaping of a concave form in wood will require considerable care. Practise on a small piece of wood about 30 × 60 mm. Without any preliminary marking out, try to make an evenly sloped hollow from opposite directions until the cuts meet in the centre. 1 cm depth will be sufficient.

There is a difficulty in carving hollows where the fibres of the grain cross (**X**). Here are two solutions to this problem:

1 Cut lightly at right angles to the grain with a very sharp tool in the area marked **X**.

2 Slice sideways with the gouge moving slightly forwards with the grain – this will produce a diagonal cutting action and will often clear the awkward fibres. Younger hands find this method manageable.

Making a small bowl

When you have achieved a satisfactory hollow on your practice piece, try making a small bowl. Use a close-grained wood such as lime or mahogany if possible – and a No. 6 or 7 gouge (see page viii).

1 Prepare a few sketches in proportion to your piece of wood – a piece about 30 × 16 cm would be suitable for a first attempt. Allow extra 3–4 cm beyond one end for holding by clamp or vice. Enlarge your most satisfactory sketch to fit the wood excluding the clamping/holding end. Note that two shapes should be drawn; an inner shape and an outer. The outer shape should touch all four sides of the wood: the hollow is carved from the inner line.

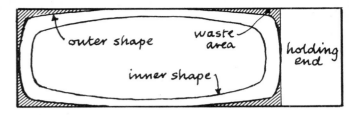

2 Transfer the design to your piece of wood. To do this, either cut out the outer and then the inner shape and draw round each in turn – or insert a piece of carbon paper between the sketch and the wood and draw over the outlines.

3 Carve out the hollow by cutting inwards from the outline of the inner shape. Use the same technique as on the practice piece, cutting into about two-thirds of the thickness of the wood. When the hollow has been completed, remove the corners of waste wood round the outer shape with a tenon or hand saw.

Shaping the underside

1 Turn over the hollowed wood and fix at the waste (holding) end with a clamp. Alternatively, have a bench stop fixed along the middle of the working surface – the work can be pushed against this as an alternative to clamping. But this is a more difficult method for young hands.

2 Mark out a base approximately half the size of the wood (excluding the waste piece).

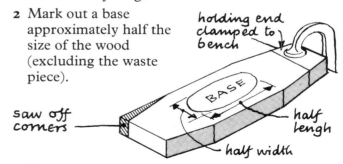

3 Start carving at the unclamped end and work gradually from this base towards the ends and sides. It is important to form a *convex* curve to complement the *concave* hollow. Develop the curve as follows:

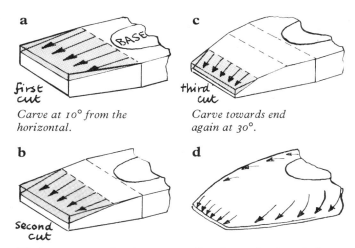

a

first cut

Carve at 10° from the horizontal.

b

Second cut

Work nearer to end and carve at 20°.

c

third cut

Carve towards end again at 30°.

d

Complete end and work down sides in direction of arrows.

4 Saw the waste end (base of bowl uppermost) to 3 mm from underside. Carve the convex curve as in **3** as far down as the saw cut goes, then round the sides as in **3d**. Finally saw off the holding piece.

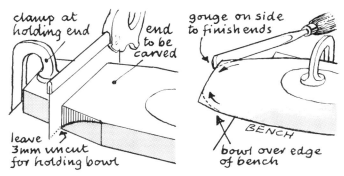

clamp at holding end

end to be carved

leave 3mm uncut for holding bowl

gouge on side to finish ends

BENCH

bowl over edge of bench

Finishing

Round off the underside to equalise the edge thickness all round to about 2 mm. The bowl can be held in a vice or clamped to the bench with the edge to be worked overhanging. Whichever way you choose, hold with a light pressure to prevent splitting. Work always in the grain direction – usually from centre side to centre end.

The inside hollow should be carefully rounded out and may be sanded smooth if required.

The whole bowl, or just the inside hollow, can be stained, varnished or polished to taste.

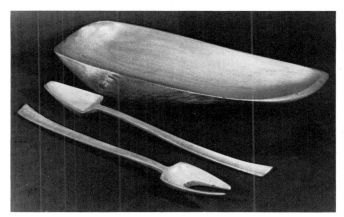

Salad bowl with a pair of servers in lime wood, finished with three coats of polyurethane varnish. (The carving of servers is shown in the illustration below.)

Development of the salad spoon. From right to left: spoon drawn out on wood surrounded by cuts sawn close to line; outer waste removed; roughly shaped; two finished spoons. The technique for carving the spoon is the same as a small bowl – start with the inside hollow and finish with the convex outer curve. Take care to blend in the shape of the bowl with the handle.

Right: a pair of butter pats and a salad spoon carved from scrap oak. A 'v' gouge has been used on topsides of the butter pats.

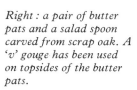

THIN PLANKS AND PLYWOOD: Layering

Use different thicknesses of wood from veneer and thin plywood to thick planking. Choose woods of different colours in order to create contrast between the layers.

1 Start with a fairly large piece of plank. Draw on it the rough outline of your chosen shape and cut it out by fretsaw, jigsaw or a bandsaw in a woodwork shop. The example sketched here of a duck shape will form the central layer to which the other layers will eventually be attached.

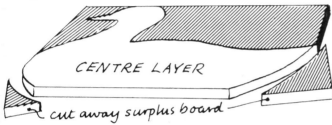

2 Draw round the cut-out duck shape on to a sheet of paper. Then draw progressively smaller duck shapes within this outline.

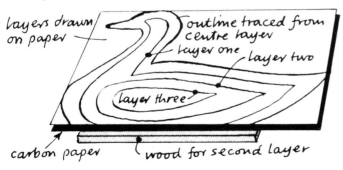

Transfer the outline of each layer twice on to wood of the same colour by drawing over the paper and through carbon paper.

3 Cut out the six extra layers, glue them with PVA adhesive and clamp all the layers together in the correct sequence and position. Ensure that glue covers every part of each surface before firmly clamping with vice or G-clamps. Leave overnight. The layering will then be ready for shaping.

4 The finished form is achieved by working with a Surform shaper plane (curved blades are most useful), rasp, file and finally sandpaper. A coating or two of varnish will bring out the colour contrasts between the layers.

Fishes, ducks and similar simple forms are relatively easy to shape and cut. Animals with legs require more care and thought in the positioning of the limbs. In the example here of a bull, the legs are formed within the second layer from the centre on each side – thus giving a firm base to the animal.

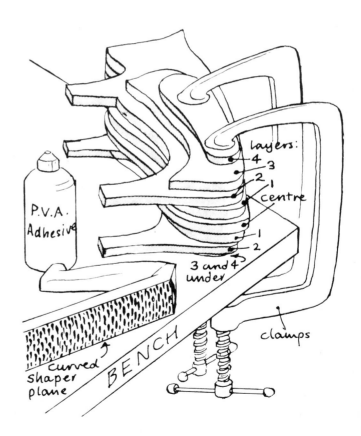

The bull layers cut out, glued and clamped together in correct layering position.

The two shapes described on the opposite page. Note the stepped effect of layers on the duck. The bull has less of this effect because of its basic squareness.

Layered or laminated bowls

Bowls and platters of layered construction are ideal projects for those who have small wood-turning lathes. The technique of wood-turning is described in many books.

Use different woods to create a wide range of colour and texture in the bands or segments.

Layered construction

The drawing below shows alternating layers of oak and mahogany in a bowl of 300 mm diameter. First build the shape by 'stepping out' the block that forms each layer – before turning.

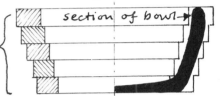

five wood 'rings', some built from two or more segments – glue with P.V.A. adhesive

section of bowl →

Segmented construction

A small bowl 120 mm across × 75 deep is built on a base plate from segments sawn in regular or irregular shapes.

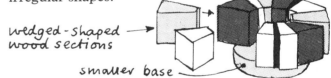

wedged-shaped wood sections

smaller base

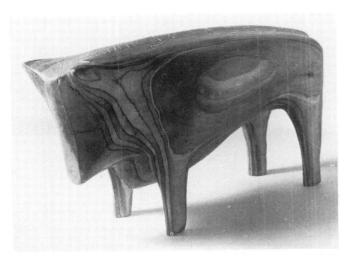

The finished bull: note the absence of detail. It is important to find the essential form and line of a figure and not to lose it in a mass of detail.

Three examples of layered or segmented bowls. The small bowl has the segments rough-turned before the final shape is produced.

PLYWOOD OFFCUTS: Layering

Another and simple form of layering is achieved by shaping pieces of thick plywood (seven or more layers) – taking advantage of this ready-made layer board.

When using plywood in this way, work on only one side – giving the effect of relief. Two or more boards can be glued together if you require sufficient thickness to work in the round from both sides.

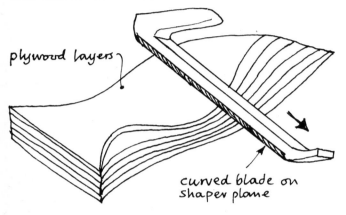

Cut out your shape (fish, bird or beast) and clamp down to the bench at one end. Use one of the Surform shaper planes or a rasp. Finish with a file or sandpaper. Finally apply a coat of wax or varnish to bring out the contrasting colours of the layers.

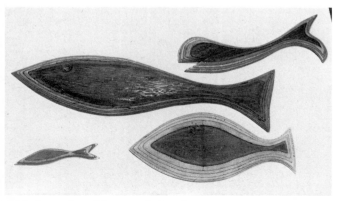

Fish forms shaped from 7-ply board.

SHAVINGS

Shavings can be collected from the floor of any woodworking shop or they can be made from wood not useful for other purposes. Adjust your plane blade to slice off a clean even layer from the edge of any 20–25 mm thick plank. The blade must be razor sharp.

Wheels
Shavings can be curved round to make circles. Wrap long shavings round a variety of mugs and other containers and glue the ends together with PVA adhesive. Slide off when dry and repeat the process as often as necessary. Small circles can be glued within large ones. Many patterns can be created in this way.

Cones and helices
Lightly coiled long shavings can be pulled gently from the centre into cones. Vary the height and width of these, and also the colours of the shavings.

Collages
Loops, wheels and spirals, tightly packed or loosely arranged within design areas, can be very effective for large collages. Conurbations, forests, complex wheels and cogs, all kinds of projects can be attempted.

Hair styles
Some amusement can be drawn from the use of shavings for hair styles – either for a character study (as shown on the right) or to create period styles.

Wheels : use different colours of wood and sizes of circle.

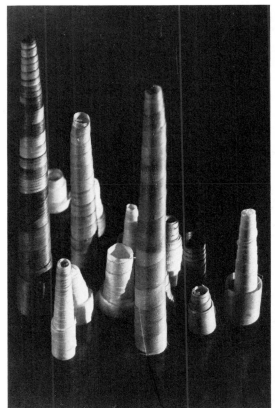

Cones and helices

A somewhat disgruntled expression – touch form and shavings.

Collage : use thick shavings or strips of veneer for the divisions.

ROOTS, DEADWOOD, DRIFTWOOD, ETC.

Debris from the seashore, from wood and forest, or from the sides of streams – all of it can contribute to art forms if careful thought is given to the found shape. The three forms on this page may be starting points for the use of roots, dead branches or driftwood. Small animal carvings could be placed on the large root – or it could itself make a splendid monster!

Sea-worn root – vision of a sea-monster's head? Or a suitable perch for a bird or animal?

Another root form – the many arms of the octopus? Or a piece of found sculpture in its own right?

A piece of dead gorse, with small balsa wood birds pinned onto the ends of thorns.

Paper and card

2

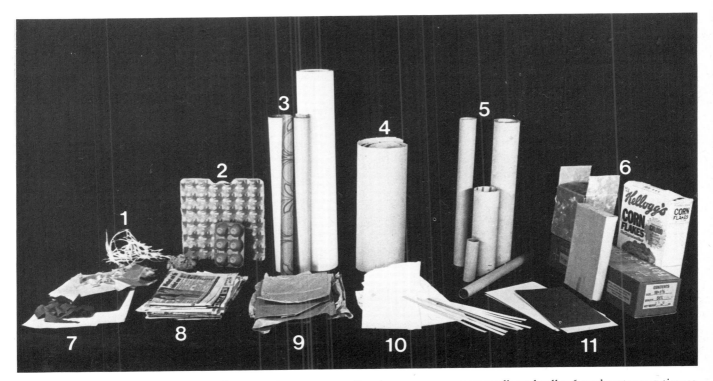

1 shredded paper; 2 pulp cartons; 3 wallpaper and newspaper roll ends; 4 sugar paper; 5 cardboard rolls; 6 card cartons; 7 tissues, carbon paper, copy paper; 8 newspapers; 9 brown paper bags and sheets; 10 cartridge paper and strips; 11 assorted thick paper, card and board

Types of paper and card

A glance round any home, office, school or shop will show how much used and handled are many kinds of paper and card. And a momentary look into any refuse area – waste-bin, skip or rubbish dump – will also show the large amount of waste from these materials, which offer a rich harvest for all potential craft enthusiasts.

Thin papers
Tissue, crêpe, carbon paper, thin copy paper, cellophane, sweet wrappings. Offices with computers dispose of print-out paper in large quantities; manufacturers of party and Christmas decorations can provide interesting offcuts in all colours of tissue and crêpe.

Medium-weight papers
Newsprint, writing and thin drawing paper, blotting and filter paper, sugar and pastel papers, wallpaper, wrapping paper and assorted kinds of printing paper. Newspaper offices sometimes sell ends of newsprint rolls for a small sum. Paint and DIY shops sell odd rolls of wallpaper for clearance. Printing works can supply guillotine offcuts and other waste. Anyone engaged in home decorating may be able to provide assorted oddments.

Glossy, shiny papers
Discarded colour magazines, many kinds of wrapping paper, sweet foil papers, offcuts from sticky display paper. Collect all your own waste magazines and wrapping papers, ask at printers for shiny paper offcuts – sometimes discarded as guillotine strips.

Thick, strong paper and card
Offcut of cartridge drawing paper and watercolour paper, manilla paper and card, food cartons, heavy oiled cardboard, strawboards. Try commercial art studios, display material manufacturers and greetings card manufacturers for thicker card.

Pre-formed papers
Paper doilies, shredded office paper, party streamers, various paper pulp containers. Some of these are available in many homes.

Sources of supply
Try all sources of supply, using the Post Office Yellow Pages. Aim especially at the larger wholesalers who often make a generous response if you can say that you work with schools or youth clubs.

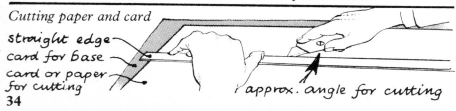

Cutting paper and card
straight edge
card for base
card or paper for cutting
approx. angle for cutting

Tools and equipment
Cutting and shaping
Scissors

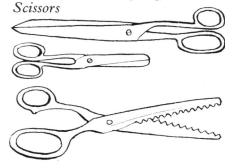

You will need long and short bladed scissors; pinking shears are useful for patterned edges.

Knives

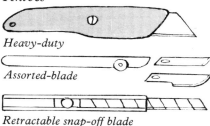

Heavy-duty

Assorted-blade

Retractable snap-off blade

'Throw-away' knife

Four basic types are shown above. It is necessary to use the heavier knife for cutting cardboard (top). The lower three are all suitable for cutting paper. Keep all blades keen by sharpening on a small oil-stone – or use the snap-off blade to have a continuously keen point.

Working surface
Always work with cardboard base pinned onto a wooden board. This can be changed as the surface becomes deeply marked. An alternative working surface is linoleum or thick plastic sheet.

Measuring and marking out

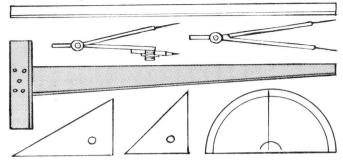

A metal ruler or straight-edge for cutting against; compasses, dividers, T-square, set-squares and protractor for precise marking out.

Folding and curling

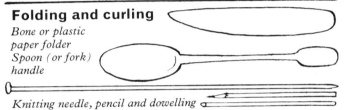

Bone or plastic
paper folder
Spoon (or fork)
handle

Knitting needle, pencil and dowelling

Many projects require careful folding of paper. A bone folder is a useful aid – or you can make one from any softwood. Shape with a knife and smooth with sandpaper. Curling and the making of cylinder shapes can be effected if paper is wrapped tightly round 'cylinders': knitting needles, pens and pencils and dowelling of different sizes.

Modelling

Two types of wooden
modelling tool: home-
made ones can be
of any softwood.

Modelling tools will be required for clay dummies if you make papier mâché masks.

Fixing (adhesives)

Cellulose or flour paste or cold-water paste for light work.

Gum and liquid glue for medium-weight work.

Copydex (latex), impact adhesive (Evo-Stik in U.K.) and self-adhesive tapes for heavier work.

Fixing (staples and fasteners)

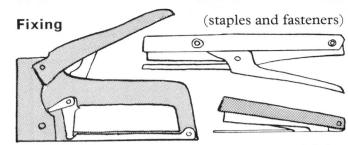

Staple gun and plier-type staplers are useful for large, heavy work, for fixing paper to backings and pinboards, and for attaching to fabrics.

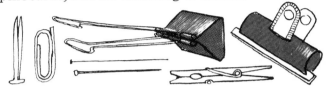

Various clips, fasteners and pins for temporary or permanent support where paper is glued or fixed to backings.

Supports

These will be needed for large projects that are not self-supporting. Three-dimensional structures and working models will require stiff card supports and possibly a wire frame.

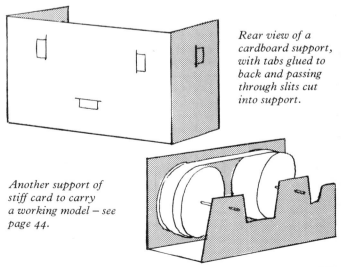

Rear view of a cardboard support, with tabs glued to back and passing through slits cut into support.

Another support of stiff card to carry a working model – see page 44.

TISSUES

Offcuts of tissue paper from paper manufacturers and decoration firms can be used for collages, or combined with inks and paints for pictures and friezes, or varnished to make transparent windows. Tissue can be cut, torn, crinkled, crumbled by crushing, soaked with water to make the colours fade, or coated with clear varnish to make it semi-transparent. Tissue can prove an attractive alternative to paint for many kinds of picture making and pattern work with the young child.

Picture making

1 Select a suitable piece of white paper or card and sketch on it in charcoal, chalk or pencil.

2 Paint the outlines of the shapes with waterproof paint or Indian ink if you wish to keep the edge as a hard line. Ordinary paint will tend to blur.

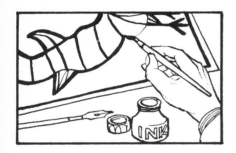

3 Mix some cellulose or flour paste and lightly brush over the areas to be covered by tissue. Cut or tear the tissue to fit the shapes and put each piece in place with a glued brush.

'The Creation' : tissue picture by 12 year old boy using red, orange and brown tissues with black Indian ink outlines.

MIXED PAPERS: Mosaics

Mosaics can make use of small squarish pieces of any thick paper or card, colour magazines, shiny paper, photographic paper, foils, etc. To produce many pieces more quickly, cut through several layers at once.

After cutting what papers you have into suitable small pieces, sort the different colours into separate piles: reds, yellows, blues, browns, etc. and sub-divide into lighter and darker groups. This will save time later, especially if you wish to paste down a large area in one or two colours only.

Prepare a backing sheet by gluing together pieces of white or coloured paper. The mosaic pieces should be glued to the backing with cellulose paste (Polycell in U.K.). A slight space may be left between squares to simulate the cement of an actual mosaic, or the piece may touch or even overlap for more intense build-up of colour.

'The Bishop', paper mosaic by 13 year old.

Below : half of a long wall mosaic of the twelve apostles for a school chapel. Various odd pieces of white paper were glued together to form twelve backing sheets 1·5 m × 50 cm. The twelve sheets were distributed among thirty 13 year old children, some of whom worked in pairs, others in groups of three or four. When the figures and names were completed, the sheets were joined together with an impact adhesive to make one long wall picture. The group then proceeded to build up the arcade framing the figures.

NDREW   MATTHEW   JAMES   SIMON   PETER   THOMAS

FLIMSY PAPERS: Cutting and folding

Thin and lightweight papers are frequently found as waste, especially print-out paper from computers. Discarded carbon paper can be useful for colour contrast against white paper. Thin strips of typist's copy paper (Bank paper) can be obtained from many small printing works. All these, and other similar, lightweight papers are ideal for decorative flowers, Christmas and party decorations and even costumes for drama work.

Note: Broken lines represent folds throughout these pages.

The illustration on the right shows a plant form made from three kinds of lightweight paper. In the centre pieces of Bank paper and carbon paper alternate; the outer tendrils are made of shredded computer print-out paper. This plant was used for an underwater scene in a school play.

The comb-like centres are made as follows:

1 Pieces of paper approx. 160 mm wide and of varying lengths are folded across the width three times.

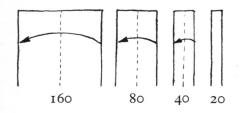

160   80   40   20

2 Cut into the folded strip with scissors from the open side to within 5 mm of the folded edge.

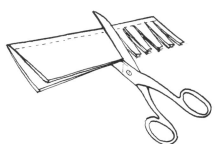

3 Open out the paper and cut as shown.

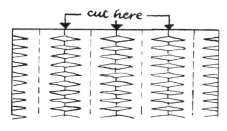

cut here

4 Four comb-like leaves result from this operation. Repeat it as many times as necessary.

STIFF PAPERS:
Cutting and folding

Any coloured or white medium or lightweight papers are suitable. Even newspaper may be used, for its print gives a pleasing texture to the pattern. A rhythmic pattern results from the folding of a sheet of paper a number of times and the cutting of a shape into this folded paper.

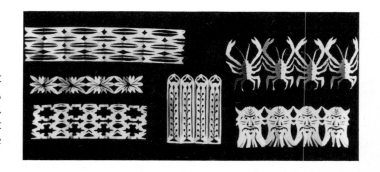

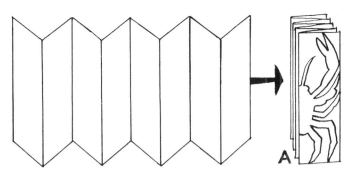

A concertina fold showing the cut-out shape for the lobster pattern which appears in the photograph at the foot of page 40. Note that the body is drawn against the fold, the outer legs on the open edge.

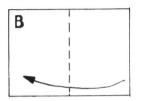

Paper can be folded as a concertina (**A**) or in half a number of times (**B**). Experiment with different kinds of folds and cuts to find out how to achieve a variety of shapes which remain joined together.

Free-standing patterns can be made by joining the ends together. This design could be folded again (on the broken line) and a half figure cut out.

Flat patterns (rather like doilies) will emerge from folding and cutting and can be made round or square. They can be mounted on a flat contrasting background – black against white, dark blue against pale blue, for example. When mounted they make attractive greetings cards or, against walls, party decorations.

To make the patterns shown here, fold the paper as follows:

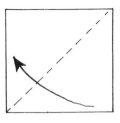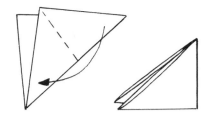

Fold a square of thin paper in half diagonally and fold again.

Cut out shape from each side leaving sufficient on edges to hold the pattern together.

A further fold will result in more repetition of the patterning:

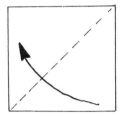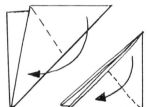

An alternation of the cut-out shape with the shape left behind in the paper can create interesting counterchange patterns.

STIFF PAPERS: Cutting and folding (continued)

All the cylindrical decorations shown here are made from a sheet of medium weight printing paper folded in half.

Lanterns

1 Fold the sheet in half and cut from the fold to within 20 mm of the open edges.

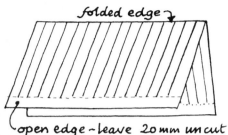

2

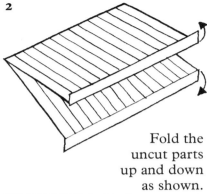

Fold the uncut parts up and down as shown.

3 Bring edges **a** and **c** to **b** and **d**. Glue or tape together.

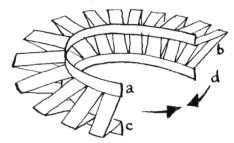

The form can now be pulled out or compressed as desired.

Stars

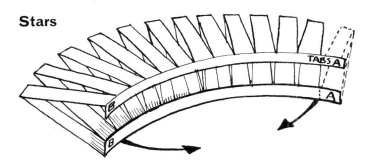

1 Start off in the same way as for the lanterns. Instead of turning the uncut edges outwards, turn them inwards and glue them together lightly. Remove one of the cut 'spokes' at **A** to make a tab.

2 The star is joined by taking tab A to the other end (B) and gluing the two ends neatly together.

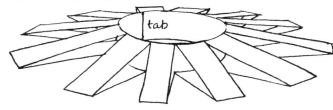

3 A deeper centre hole can be made by increasing the width of the uncut edges. Cardboard or paper cylinders can be fitted into the centre hole of several stars together to make them into decorative wheels spinning on the cylinder axis.

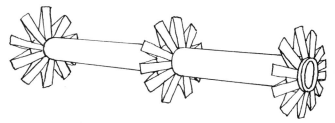

Variations of cut

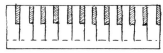

Remove shaded areas

Cut out darts

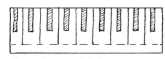

Cut slots within cuts

Have cuts very close

Experiment further

Towers

The tower structures illustrated here are made from a sheet of paper folded three times.

1 Fold down centre and each edge into centre fold.

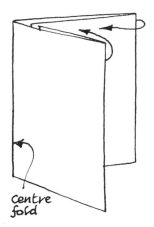

2 Draw a line 20 mm from centre fold and cut at regular intervals from outer edges.

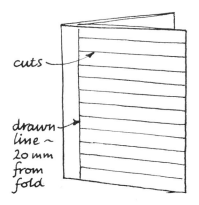

3 Open up and fold strips in alternate directions. Finally dovetail the two halves together.

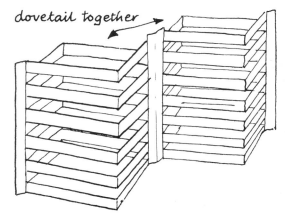

HEAVIER PAPERS: Scoring and folding

Heavier papers require scoring before folding. Score lines across paper with the tip of a knife or scissor blade, pressing gently to avoid cutting the paper. Fold paper away from score marks. In the case of concertina folds this means scoring on alternate sides of the paper.

Concertina folds

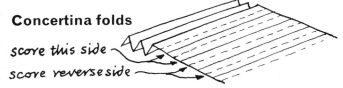

score this side
score reverse side

Fan shapes

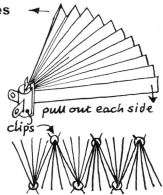

pull out each side
clips

Pleat a sheet of paper concertina-fashion. Glue between the folds at one side and hold with a clip till dry.

Alternating fan shapes Pinch together six or so folds on one side, glue and clip – then six on the other. Repeat to the end of the concertina.

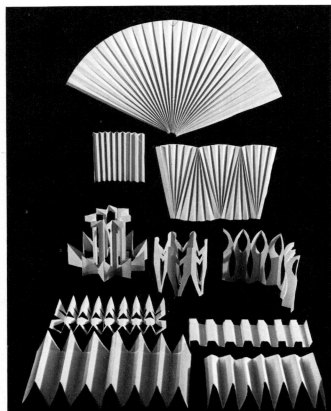

Fan shapes and various folded forms are shown above, made from offcuts of cartridge paper and oddments of silicone-backed paper. These papers are both easier to fold if scored first. The curved forms in the centre of the group are concertina folds with various shapes cut out. The crenellated form (just above bottom right) demands a greater number of scores and folds and is suitable for cog wheels.

Machines

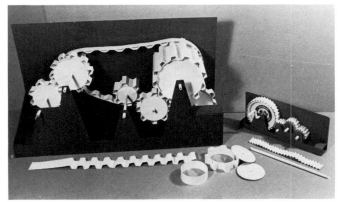

Cog wheels and belts can be made from corrugated paper (see section on Corrugated Cardboard) but otherwise cogs may be formed from strips of paper folded twice one way and twice the other to make crenellations. Glue the folded strip round a paper/card cylinder of similar width to make wheels, or onto a long strip of paper or firm fabric to make belts (in which case open out each 'cog' to a wedge shape). Axles can be made from thin dowelling or old knitting needles, driving handles of bent coathanger wire. Put a touch of impact adhesive where axles meet centre holes of wheels. Supports are of stout card.

Cogs

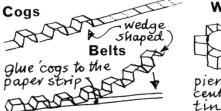

wedge shaped)

Belts

glue 'cogs to the paper strip

Wheels

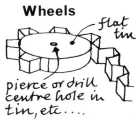

flat tin

pierce or drill centre hole in tin, etc....

LOW RELIEF TECHNIQUES:
Folding and cutting

Textured and patterned surfaces on flat sheets of scrap paper can be produced by a variety of ways: cutting, folding, punching and threading with paper strips.

These sheets can be shaped into cylinders and towers if the ends are glued together. Strong, oblique lighting will accentuate the surface treatment by casting shadows across the raised areas.

Threading strips

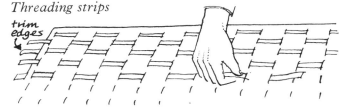

Cut regular slits into a sheet of paper with a sharp knife and interweave narrow strips of paper (of the same or a different colour) to make a basket-weave texture.

Punching

Punch holes in the paper with any kind of punch.

Experiment with a variety of folds and cut-outs.

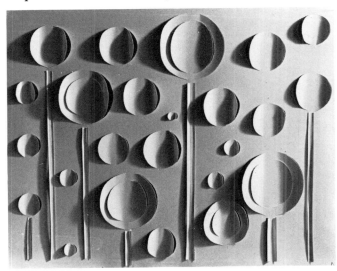

Cutting and curling up edges.

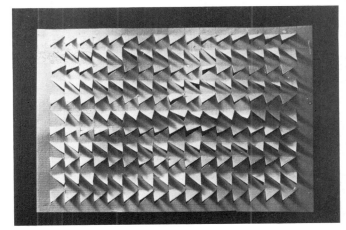

Cutting and folding over.

Sculptured reliefs

Pattern and texture can effectively suggest the surfaces of natural forms – animals, birds and fishes. Cut and fold the paper to emphasise the texture with strong side lighting. The eyes of the fish are cut on either side and the cut edges curled up. Fins are cut with scissors. Tail fin and bird's tail are lightly scored and folded.

To create deeper shadows, lift some areas slightly.

The examples illustrated here were all made from scraps of cartridge paper.

LOW RELIEF TECHNIQUES: Scoring, folding and cutting

Scoring and folding sheets of thicker paper can give an illusion of three-dimensional depth when used with strong side lighting. There is a great variety of decoration possible by this method.

Scoring straight lines

1 Score lightly with a knife tip or scissor blade point along a metal straight-edge.

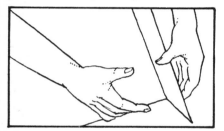

2 Fold down and away from all score lines.

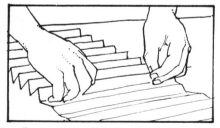

3 Lengths of pleating can be shaped on a flat surface after the first gentle folds.

Note
Pressure of scoring will vary according to the type of paper. Light paper may need no more than a pencil point – heavy papers a dull point with heavy pressure.

Cut and fold reliefs

On the following diagrams horizontal lines represent cuts with a sharp knife, vertical lines are score marks on the top side and, where broken, on the reverse side.

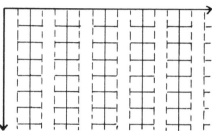

Cubed relief: one fold forward and two folds back.

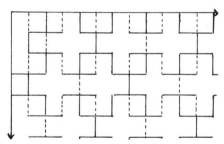

A cross-form relief: a more complex form with cuts and score marks staggered.

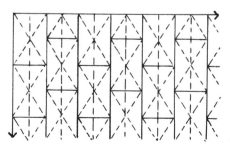

Diamond-shaped relief: lines are scored diagonally between the horizontal cuts. The blunt side of a knife blade is inserted in the centre of slits to make the folding back of the diamonds easier.

Detail of a dart relief: leave spaces between top and base of each dart. Darts are pushed in.

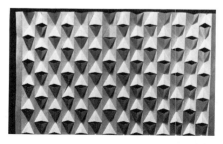

Sculptured reliefs

Curved scoring opens up a wider range of possibilities in paper relief and lends itself to strong pictorial forms. The picture relief illustrated below is made up largely from curves.

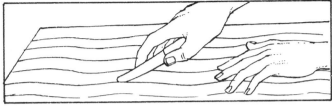

Making waves: draw wavy lines at regular intervals across the paper, then score with a dull point.

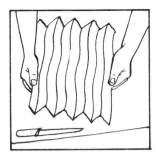

Bend alternate lines gently up and down. Do not press hard until all folds are begun.

First cut out shapes and then score along central line of each part. Try this on oddments.

PAPER SCULPTURE:

Oddments of stiff coloured papers are ideal for relief and for 'in-the-round' costume sculpture. The two relief soldiers use five colours: black for hats and boots, white for shirt and breeches, red and blue for jackets, yellow for lapels and buttons. Cuffs, hair curls are also white. Features can be drawn on faces and hands.

Relief

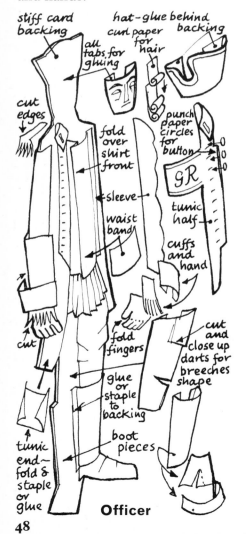

stiff card backing

all tabs for gluing

hat-glue behind backing

curl paper for hair

cut edges

fold over shirt front

sleeve

waist band

punch paper circles for button

GR

tunic half

cuffs and hand

cut

fold fingers

cut and close up darts for breeches shape

glue or staple to backing

tunic end—fold & staple or glue

boot pieces

Officer

48

Paper relief soldiers : left, a private of the New York Regiment, 1775; right, officer of the British 15th Foot Regiment, 1776. Many authentic styles of costume can be constructed from paper oddments.

Figures in the round

Cylinders and cones are the foundation for the construction of many animal and human paper figures. Larger-scale figures can be supported by card rolls.

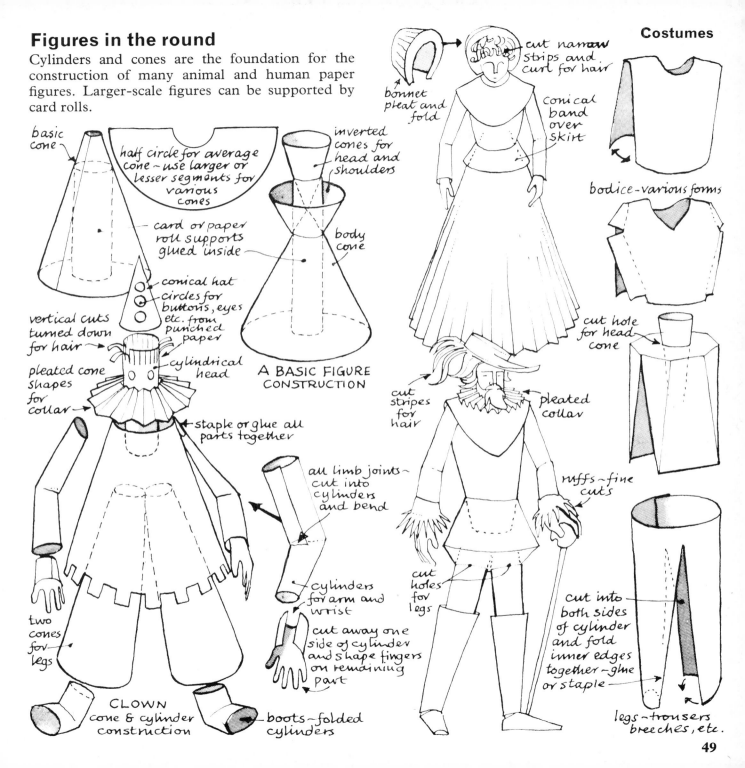

basic cone

half circle for average cone – use larger or lesser segments for various cones

card or paper roll supports glued inside

conical hat

circles for buttons, eyes etc. from punched paper

vertical cuts turned down for hair

pleated cone shapes for collar

cylindrical head

inverted cones for head and shoulders

body cone

A BASIC FIGURE CONSTRUCTION

staple or glue all parts together

all limb joints – cut into cylinders and bend

cylinders for arm and wrist

cut away one side of cylinder and shape fingers on remaining part

two cones for legs

CLOWN
cone & cylinder construction

boots – folded cylinders

cut narrow strips and curl for hair

bonnet pleat and fold

conical band over skirt

bodice – various forms

cut hole for head cone

cut stripes for hair

pleated collar

ruffs – fine cuts

cut holes for legs

cut into both sides of cylinder and fold inner edges together – glue or staple

legs – trousers breeches, etc.

49

LARGE GROUP PROJECTS 1

Wall and window displays are frequently constructed from paper and card. Large-scale displays are ideal for group projects. Members of a group can each develop separate parts that contribute to a common theme. But they should first discuss plans: which subject, methods to be employed, the space necessary, responsibility for the background scene, choice of characters or objects against it, and so on. The underwater scene illustrated here is an example of this kind of project. Construction of the rocks, plants and sea creatures can involve up to 20 or more people. The following pages show the construction methods for the larger forms.

Shellfish

Any sea creature such as a crab, lobster or shrimp which consists of many parts should first be studied from photographs, drawings or from life. Then experiment with scraps of stiff paper.

The lobster illustrated right is made up of 43 parts: 24 for the eight legs, 8 for the pincers, 8 for the body and 3 for the tail.

Most parts are of cylinder or cone construction, with pleated fan shapes for the tail. The exploded view (below) of the parts shows cuts, folds and fixing points.

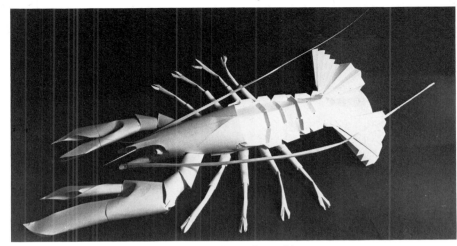

Paper sculpture lobster made from scrap pieces of cartridge.

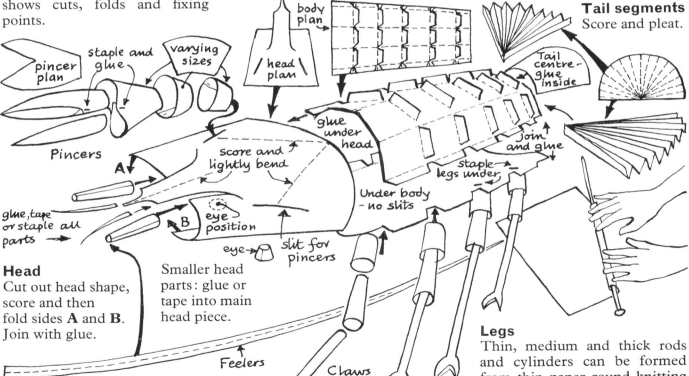

body plan

head plan

Tail segments
Score and pleat.

Tail centre - glue inside

glue under head

Join and glue

staple legs under

Under body - no slits

Pincers

pincer plan

staple and glue

varying sizes

score and lightly bend

eye position

eye

slit for pincers

A

B

glue, tape or staple all parts →

Head
Cut out head shape, score and then fold sides **A** and **B**. Join with glue.

Smaller head parts: glue or tape into main head piece.

Feelers

Long feelers
Cut long narrow curved shape and score along centre line. Fold lightly to make rigid.

Claws

Flatten rod end and cut centre ~ open and cut claws

Legs
Thin, medium and thick rods and cylinders can be formed from thin paper round knitting needles, pencils and dowelling. Roll on paper diagonally, cut along the length of the roll and glue down.

LARGE GROUP PROJECTS 2

Turtle

By comparison with the more complex forms on the previous page, the turtle (or tortoise or similar) is simple in shape and number of parts. The interest lies more in the pattern within the shape and depends more on careful scoring and folding. The illustrations explain the patterning.

The head is a basic cylinder with cuts and folds – with an additional piece for the jaw and another for the neck join.

All parts are of scrap cartridge except the shell. This is of stiff card. If a large piece is not available, smaller pieces can be joined along the pattern shapes.

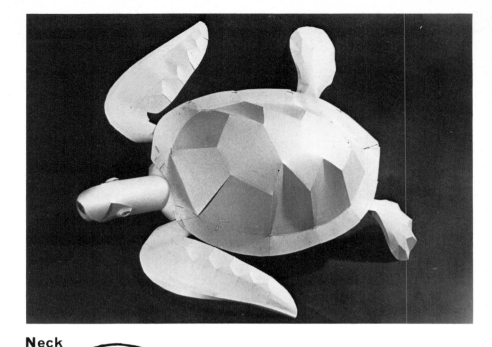

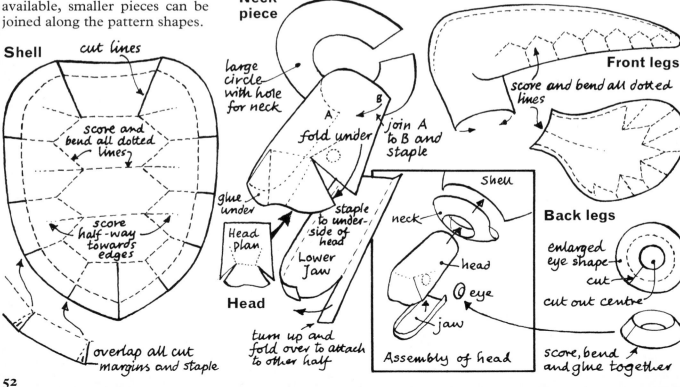

Shell
cut lines
score and bend all dotted lines
score half-way towards edges
overlap all cut margins and staple

Neck piece
large circle with hole for neck
A   B
fold under
join A to B and staple
glue under
staple to underside of head
Head plan
Lower Jaw
Head
turn up and fold over to attach to other half

neck
Shell
head
eye
jaw
Assembly of head

Front legs
score and bend all dotted lines

Back legs
enlarged eye shape
cut
cut out centre
score, bend and glue together

Fish and plants

Fish and plants are so various in shape that they offer considerable scope for paper sculpture.

The decorative fish on the right uses cone shapes for the head and body, triangles for the tail and fin. The interest again lies in the surface treatment: scales cut and bent forward on the body, fin and tail pleated, mouth and gill fins curved, scored and folded. By contrast, the head has a plain surface.

See page 47 for the wave backing.

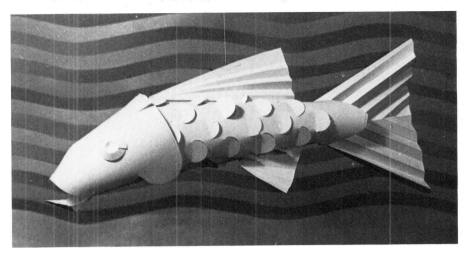

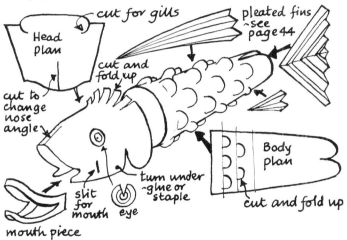

Starfish
Cut out flat shapes, lightly score along centre of each arm and fold down edges. Add pattern and texture by either punching holes or gluing on punch waste or, for very large models, attaching miniature cones.

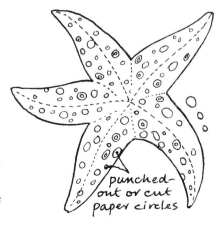

punched-out or cut paper circles

Smaller fish

Simple cut-out shapes (see scene on page 50) can be cut 3 or 4 at a time on thin paper – lightly score and fold.

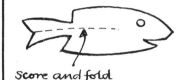

score and fold

Jellyfish
Cut out a spiral shape from a circle. Starting from centre, glue edges into more of a cone. Use sticky tape underneath to strengthen.

shreaded paper or very narrow strips of cut paper

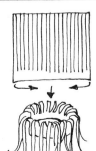

Plants (sea anemones)
Cut squares of thin paper into very narrow strips to within 25 mm of other side. Join ends of uncut side together and let the strips tumble about.

Vary this technique by using different papers, cutting strips of varying width, inserting one kind into another, etc.

STIFF PAPER AND CARD:
Geometry models

Models of the five regular geometric solids can be constructed from offcuts of paper and card. A T-square, set square and protractor will be needed for the correct marking-out of the angles.

To allow the gluing of one face to another, tabs should be left on the edges of each face. This may not be necessary for thick card which can be glued without tabs.

Patterned papers or paints can be used to decorate the models. The faces may have shapes cut out before assembly.

The illustrations show a variety of forms made from stiff paper. Such models can be made for use in displays or exhibitions – or can be made suitable for gift containers if one face is glued on one edge only, with tabs that can be tucked inside. Very large models can be built with heavy paper or card.

Plans (or nets) for five models with tabs for joining edges

The five solids are the tetrahedron (four sides), hexahedron (six sides), octahedron (eight sides), dodecahedron (twelve sides) and icosahedron (twenty sides).

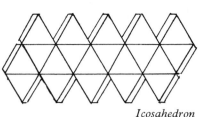

Icosahedron

Tetrahedron

Octahedron

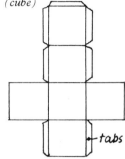

Hexahedron (cube)

←*tabs*

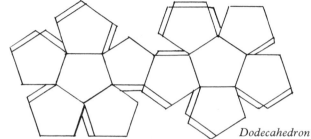

Dodecahedron

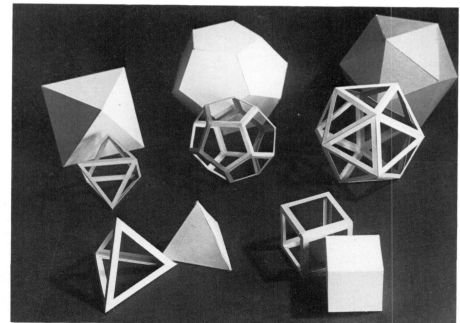

Above, models of the five regular geometric solids – some with open faces.
Left, a variety of shapes.

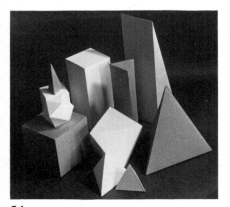

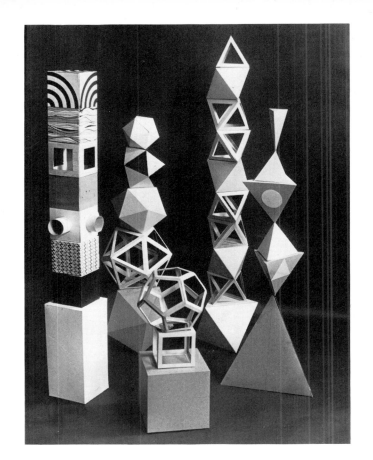

Lampshades

These can be assembled from a set of twenty equilateral triangles and decorated in a variety of ways.

1 Cut a triangle from a piece of paper and trace round it twenty times.

3 Add the remaining fifteen pieces to complete the 'solid'.

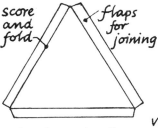

2 Staple or glue five pieces together.

4 For a lampshade one triangle should be of stiff card. Fit a lamp socket:

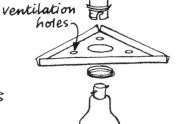

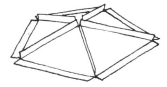

Towers

Constructions varying in shape, pattern and colour can be made by building one 'solid' on top of another to any height. Towers such as the one illustrated above right will require the support of a rigid wire.

Experiment with every kind of 'solid': use a wide range of paper offcuts (patterned and plain) and decorate by pasting patterned paper to plain models, printing techniques, brush or pen work, paint, the cutting-out of shapes within the faces, and the additon of other parts through holes in the faces (see the example of the tower illustrated above left).

Assemblages of this kind make interesting group projects in schools – whether or not in connection with mathematics. Each child can select a different 'solid' or invent his own.

Lampshades: variations made by the cutting of holes.

PAPER PRINTING

An interesting printing method involves the use of cut or torn scrap paper glued to a firm, flat surface and rolled with printing ink. The raised pieces of paper (or card) and the accidental textures from surfaces between the pieces can create many lively printing effects.

Making a paper print

1 Paper can be torn, sliced into rectangles or squares with a craft knife, or cut into curved shapes with scissors.

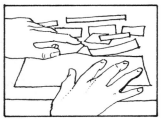 

Straight cuts   *Curved cuts*

2 Glue down the pieces onto a stiff card with a strong adhesive – gum or impact glue.

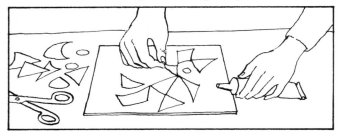

3 Roll out the printing ink (linoleum ink is ideal) on a piece of hardboard or glass. Then roll the ink over the surface of the 'printing block' with an even pressure in all directions.

Rolling out ink   *Rolling ink on block*

4 Lay a piece of printing paper carefully on the inked surface. With a clean roller, work carefully in all directions over the paper. Lift one corner of the paper to see if the design is coming out clearly – repeat the rolling if necessary.

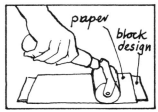 

Roll with a clean roller   *Lift paper to see if design is sharp*

Stencil prints

Instead of printing from a raised surface block, cut a stencil from thin card and lay it over the printing paper. If the stencil is shifted about, a repeated pattern can be made.

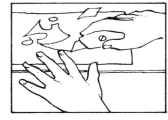 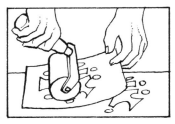

Cutting a stencil   *Repeating the print*

Animated prints

Cut out the parts of a figure: head, torso, upper and lower arms and legs, feet and hands. Overlap at joints, fix with small metal fasteners and flatten with a hammer. This figure can be adjusted to any position of the limbs. Print off in a series of positions to make a cartoon strip.

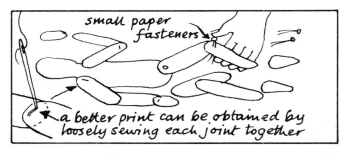

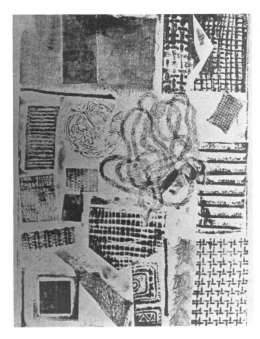

Above, a widely spaced card print 40 cm × 30 cm with the ink showing up the textured background between shapes.

Above, printing from various embossed papers and oddments – an experimental print by an 11 year old exploring the possibilities of pattern and texture. 20 cm × 30 cm.

Below, two animated card prints by 14 year olds. The pivoted limbs allow a sequence of body movement. Each joint is sewn with cotton.

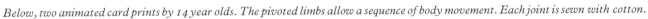

PAPIER MÂCHÉ

Papier mâché, using newspapers with flour or cellulose wallpaper paste, is very strong and ideal for a large range of modelling forms.

Prepare a large bowl of paste and soak strips of paper roughly 150 × 80 mm. Apply these strips to shaped wire frames. About five layers are sufficient for a strong surface which can be painted when dry.

Portrait models

Such models will require a framework made from wire or wood.

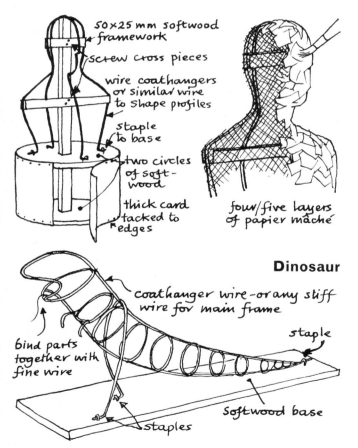

50×25 mm softwood framework

screw cross pieces

wire coathangers or similar wire to shape profiles

staple to base

two circles of softwood

thick card tacked to edges

four/five layers of papier mâché

Dinosaur

coathanger wire - or any stiff wire for main frame

staple

bind parts together with fine wire

staples

softwood base

The framework is of stiff wire stapled to a wooden base and covered with wire mesh. A small model can be made without mesh if pieces of stiff paper are glued round the wire before papier mâché is added.

Carnival heads

The framework for large heads is described under Wire Mesh in the section on Metals.

Large carnival head 1 m high made from papier mâché. Hair may be added (rug wool, etc.) and the neck padded inside with plastic foam. In the background, a standing figure made from papier mâché.

Portrait bust 1·1 m high made by two 14 year olds and a dinosaur 1·2 m long made by a group of 8 year olds. The modelling on the base of the bust is done with paper pulp (see facing page).

PAPER PULP

Newspapers, discarded sugar paper and other soft papers can be soaked or boiled to make a pulp for modelling. With the addition of paste and a filler, this pulp is similar to modelling clay and sets very hard. It can then be sanded smooth, painted or varnished. It will shrink slightly when thoroughly dry.

The mixture
Tear the paper into small pieces. Any utensil will serve for soaking, a galvanised bucket or metal bowl will be necessary for boiling. Leave for a few hours before beating or thumping with a stout stick in order to break down the fibres.

When the mixture is well soaked or cool, squeeze out the excess water and knead to break down lumps. Mix in some flour or cellulose paste to make a thick wet pulp and gradually sprinkle with a filler (builder's plaster or whiting) until the pulp has a clay-like consistency.

Using paper pulp
Relief landscapes or fairly low modelling can be done direct onto a wooden base. Large models will require a support – fine wire mesh is suitable.

Gargoyles
The examples shown on the right are supported on frameworks of wire mesh stapled to wooden wall plates and bases.

Above, five gargoyles made by 14 year olds.

Below, close-up of one gargoyle to show the detailed modelling.

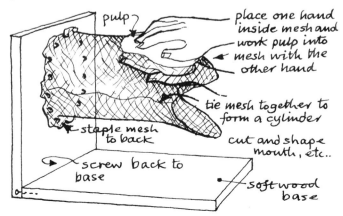

Comedy mask

Cartoon cat face

SCRAP CARD AND STIFF PAPER: Masks

An endless variety of masks can be made from scrap card and stiff paper. A little ingenuity and imagination can produce many colourful characters from a minimum of materials. Foils, fabrics and plastics can be added, also paint, to add texture and pattern to the basic shapes. The card from cornflake packets will be sufficient for many simple masks – larger pieces of card will be needed for more elaborate masks.

Comedy mask

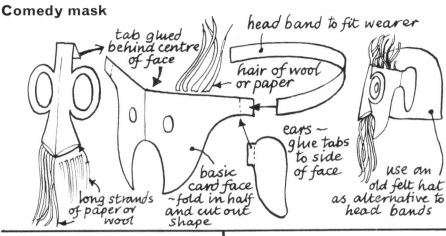

tab glued behind centre of face

head band to fit wearer

hair of wool or paper

long strands of paper or wool

basic card face ~ fold in half and cut out shape

ears ~ glue tabs to side of face

use an old felt hat as alternative to head bands

Cat mask

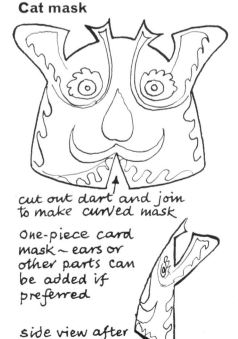

cut out dart and join to make curved mask

One-piece card mask ~ ears or other parts can be added if preferred

side view after joining dart →

Fire god

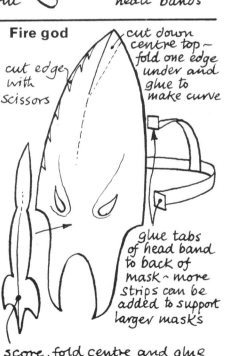

cut down centre top ~ fold one edge under and glue to make curve

cut edge with scissors

glue tabs of head band to back of mask ~ more strips can be added to support larger masks

score, fold centre and glue to mask

Fire god

Masks and accessories

Elaborate, colourful costume masks can be made from all kinds of paper scrap. The head of Neptune for a dance drama was made from cartridge, thin card (from cornflake packets), offcuts of foil paper, shredded computer print-out paper, a few pieces of plastic net and a few drinking straws.

Head of Neptune

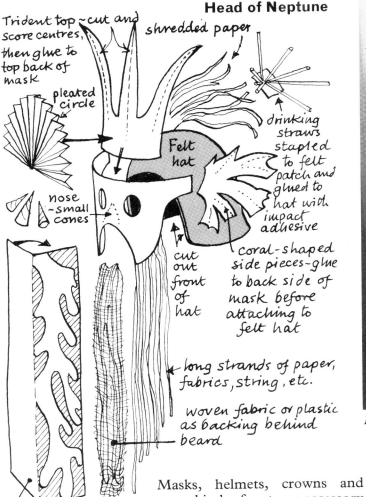

Trident top ~ cut and score centres, then glue to top back of mask

shredded paper

pleated circle

drinking straws stapled to felt patch and glued to hat with impact adhesive

Felt hat

nose ~ small cones

cut out front of hat

coral-shaped side pieces ~ glue to back side of mask before attaching to felt hat

long strands of paper, fabrics, string, etc.

woven fabric or plastic as backing behind beard

beard ~ fold length of paper in half and cut seaweed shape ~ open out and glue to lower back side of mask

Head of Neptune

Masks, helmets, crowns and many kinds of costume accessory can be made from paper for plays or carnivals. Use strong paper and add any oddments to suit the design. Always consider the colour scheme, pattern and texture.

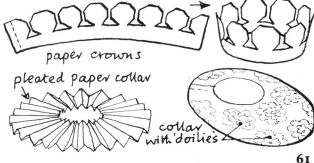

paper crowns

pleated paper collar

collar with doilies

CARDBOARD MODELS:
Buildings

Geometry models are the basis of buildings of all shapes and sizes. The overhanging storeys on the medieval buildings shown below were made from an assortment of cereal and other food containers by a class of young children.

Box buildings

Sheets of cardboard can be turned into buildings if plans and elevations are drawn and then cut out with tabs.

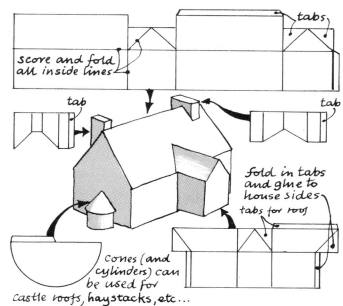

glue tab under

glue tabs under roof

ROOF BASE

TAB

ROOF BASE

paper pasted round box

food containers
(use paint or pasted papers for tiles, boarding stones, bricks, etc.)

score and fold all inside lines

tabs

tab

tab

fold in tabs and glue to house sides

tabs for roof

cones (and cylinders) can be used for castle roofs, haystacks, etc...

Wall collage of cardboard relief buildings with cut-out paper figure and animals. The whole collage has been decorated with paint and potato prints. (This collage was a group project by 9–10 year olds.)

Scale models

Scale models for stage and architectural design can be built from scrap card oddments. The model illustrated below was made from mounting board offcuts, cereal packets and some pieces of balsa wood (which could have been replaced by card). The base and backing was made from oddments of hardboard and cardboard.

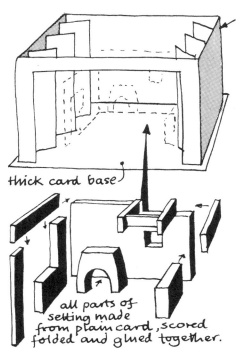

thick card base

all parts of setting made from plain card, scored folded and glued together.

stage model theatre made from thick cardboard to accommodate various stage settings.

Stage model design for 'Amahl and the Night Visitors' by Carlo Menotti.

HEAVY CARDBOARD

Totem pole

It is sometimes possible to obtain offcuts of the very thick, heavy cardboard used in the upholstery trade for modern furniture. A totem pole made from such card was glued and tacked to a wooden frame. All the features are of card, corrugated card and felt. The totem was finally covered with plastic emulson paint – poster paint would be an alternative.

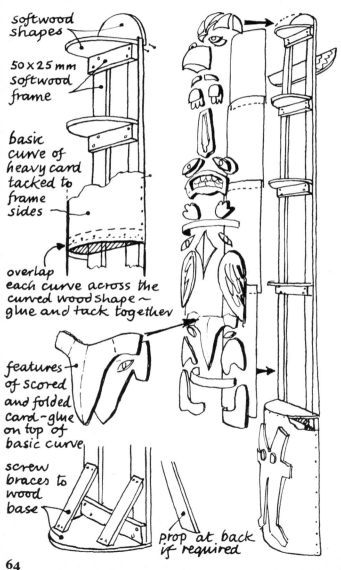

softwood shapes

50 x 25 mm softwood frame

basic curve of heavy card tacked to frame sides

overlap each curve across the curved wood shape ~ glue and tack together

features of scored and folded card - glue on top of basic curve

screw braces to wood base

prop at back if required

Corrugated cardboard 3

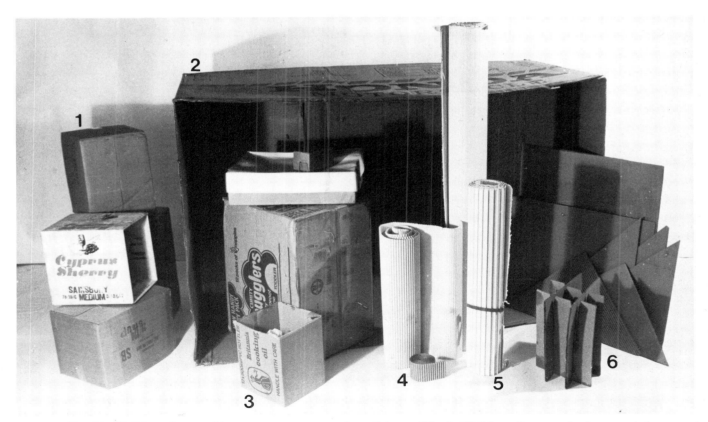

1 cartons (Double Wall board); 2 packing cases; 3 cartons and small boxes (Single Wall board); 4 standard corrugated paper; 5 decorative corrugated paper; 6 carton separators and offcuts

CORRUGATED CARDBOARD
The material

After newspaper, corrugated cardboard is perhaps the most readily available material. It is discarded in vast quantities by most department stores, retailers and wholesalers. Look down or behind any main shopping street before the refuse van collects – the variety of box, carton and loose packing is enormous.

Shopkeepers are often delighted to let you have such material provided that you collect it and do so as quickly as possible. But they will often keep particular types or sizes for you.

Four types of corrugated cardboard are manufactured (manufacturers usually term it fibreboard):

1 Corrugated card, sometimes called 'corrugated paper', is a lightweight, flexible material with two layers – one fluted and the other flat. It is used chiefly as packing material within a carton.

2 Single Wall corrugated card is built of three layers – the fluted layer is enclosed between two flat layers. This is the most common of the four types and is found in abundance through the retail food trade, usually for small to medium sized cartons. It is sometimes referred to as American Board in the U.K.

3 Double Wall corrugated card has five layers (two fluted, one thinner than the other, set between three flat). This is used for the containers of large refrigerators and of motor cycles – also for heavy objects in smaller sizes. A stronger type has two equal flutings with thicker outer layers (Duaboard in U.K.).

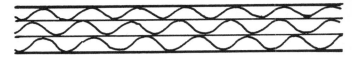

4 Triple Wall corrugated card is made similarly but with seven layers. This is a heavyweight packing material used by exporters. ('Tri-board' in U.K.)

Tools and equipment

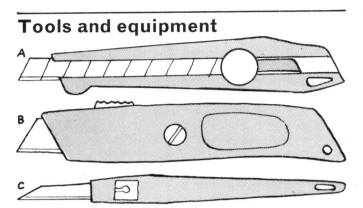

The essential tool for corrugated cardboard is a permanently sharp craft knife. The ideal knife for this purpose has a break-off blade (**A**). The standard trimming knife is also suitable (**B**) but needs frequent sharpening. Both types have retractable blades – essential for work with young children. A cheap 'throwaway' knife (**C**) is now on the market: once it is blunt it is thrown away but, in fact, it can, with care, be sharpened two or three times. The use of a cardboard cutting base will help retain the cutting point of all knife blades.

Scissors can be useful, especially for young children.

A cutting edge should be of steel (either a steel rule or a longer steel straight-edge).

Adhesives are no problem – even flour paste can be used though it is slow to dry. For quick drying results (always desirable for large group work) use PVA adhesive diluted with water in a proportion of 1:1. Cellulose adhesive of a thick consistency can also be used satisfactorily with the material.

Pieces of thin dowelling or cane, or old knitting needles are useful for axles between pieces of card. See pages 80–81.

Preparation

When selecting card for craft-work, look for clean, smooth boxes only as when crushed this card becomes useless. The surface finish may be important: matt surfaced card is needed for the soaking technique that separates layer from layer. (See Machines on page 78.)

Keep a few large cartons on one side for the storage of assorted pieces of card. Particularly for large group work prepare a wide variety of shapes, sizes, types, etc., a few strips with the fluting revealed.

The basic problem with a comparatively new craft material is that there are no traditional techniques for handling it. Corrugated cardboard is an awkward, rigid material and ways have to be found to cut and manipulate it in quantity.

A number of projects are illustrated on the following pages that exploit some of the particular properties of the material. With practice and experiment, one may find many new ways of developing its uses.

If you wish to prepare a quantity of strips (approximately 15 × 300 mm is a convenient size to begin with), first mark cutting lines with the strip length made parallel to fluting.

To cut the card, lay rule or straight-edge at right angle to the line of the fluting and hold it down firmly. Cut vertically down to the cutting board with the knife.

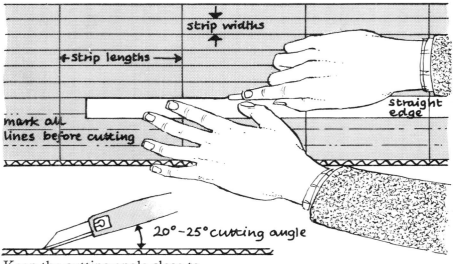

Keep the cutting angle close to the board for a smooth, clean cut.

If you wish to make wheels and driving belts for moving mechanisms (see page 78) it will be necessary to use corrugated paper or to peel off one plain layer from a piece of Single Wall card. This may or may not be difficult: moisten or soak until the plain layer can be peeled away. The fluting can be strengthened by varnishing or painting. *Note*: cut out your strip of card *before* peeling off.

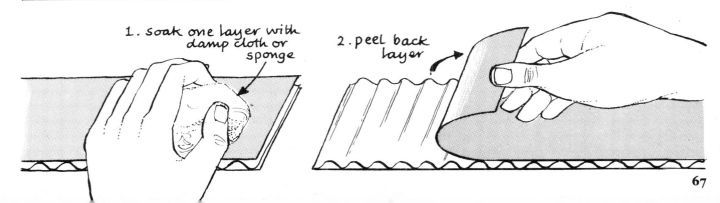

1. soak one layer with damp cloth or sponge

2. peel back layer

A home-made cutting machine

If corrugated cardboard is to be used as a major craft material, it will be necessary to cut large quantities of strips. Imagine a class of twenty, each member needing twenty strips, and then multiply by the number of classes – the quantity required would be enormous and the cutting of them would take too much time. In such a situation it is practical to build a cutting machine along the lines of the one illustrated below. This is very simple and something more complicated could be devised. This machine cuts twelve strips at a time, 750 mm long × 15 mm wide. The card can be cut completely through or not – this will depend upon the projects that you have in mind.

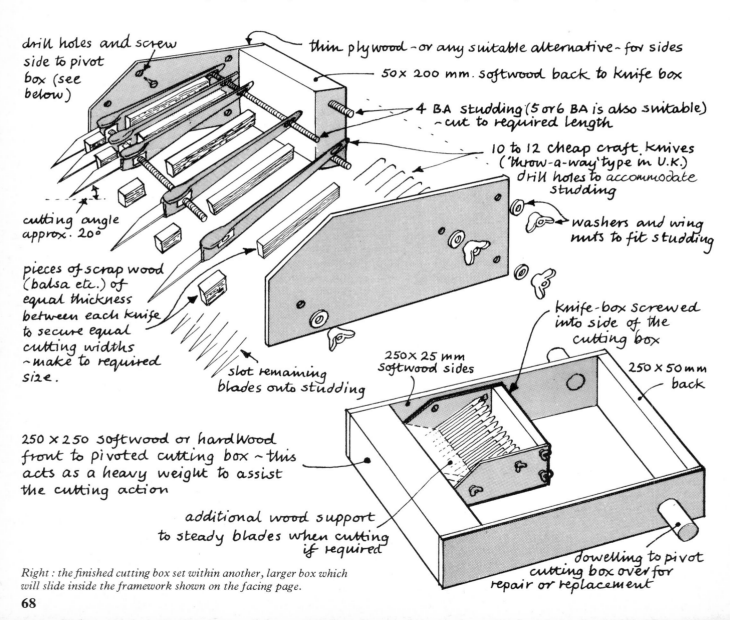

drill holes and screw side to pivot box (see below)

thin plywood – or any suitable alternative – for sides

50 × 200 mm. softwood back to knife box

4 BA studding (5 or 6 BA is also suitable) – cut to required length

10 to 12 cheap craft knives ('throw-a-way' type in U.K.) drill holes to accommodate studding

cutting angle approx. 20°

washers and wing nuts to fit studding

pieces of scrap wood (balsa etc.) of equal thickness between each knife to secure equal cutting widths – make to required size.

slot remaining blades onto studding

knife-box screwed into side of the cutting box

250 × 25 mm softwood sides

250 × 50 mm back

250 × 250 softwood or hardwood front to pivoted cutting box – this acts as a heavy weight to assist the cutting action

additional wood support to steady blades when cutting if required

dowelling to pivot cutting box over for repair or replacement

Right : the finished cutting box set within another, larger box which will slide inside the framework shown on the facing page.

The cutting frame

This shows the sliding/cutting box set within the larger cutting frame. The card for cutting is laid on the bed of the frame and the cutter drawn across.

The number of cutters is optional but extra pressure will be needed the more cutters there are.

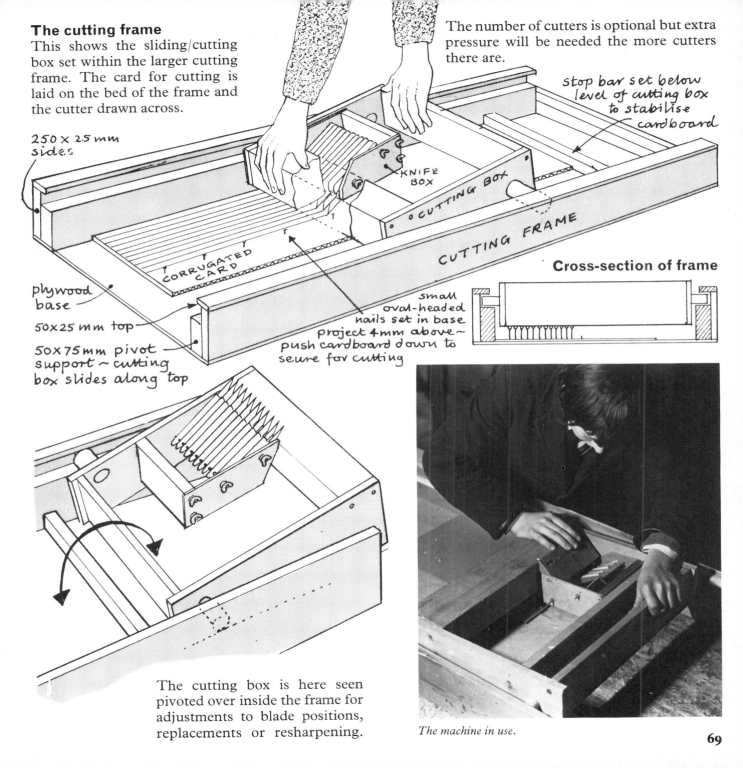

stop bar set below level of cutting box to stabilise cardboard

250 x 25 mm sides

KNIFE BOX

CUTTING BOX

CUTTING FRAME

CORRUGATED CARD

Cross-section of frame

plywood base

50 x 25 mm top

50 x 75 mm pivot support ~ cutting box slides along top

small oval-headed nails set in base project 4mm above ~ push cardboard down to secure for cutting

The cutting box is here seen pivoted over inside the frame for adjustments to blade positions, replacements or resharpening.

The machine in use.

69

Some cutting techniques

To exploit the material fully it is worth experimenting with a variety of cutting techniques. Try some of the following:

1 Vary the strips in length and width; cut strips in Single, Double or Triple Wall; glue strips together for extra thickness.

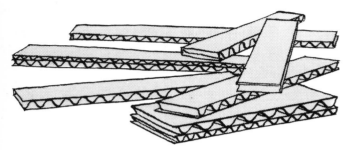

2 Cut groups of three, four or more strips, cutting right through only between groups and otherwise cutting through to leave one layer uncut. The groups can be folded into 'solids', with the sides joined inside the solid with sticky tape.

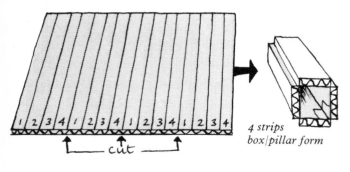

4 strips box/pillar form

3 strips

Try other polygons.

6 strips

3 You can make zig-zag forms by cutting alternately from one side of the card and then the other and leaving one layer uncut.

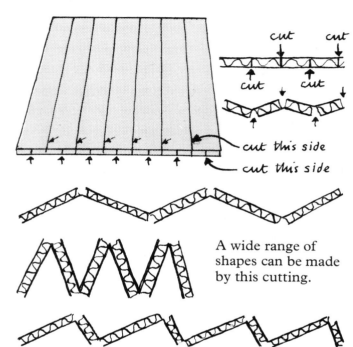

cut this side
cut this side

A wide range of shapes can be made by this cutting.

Wide and narrow strips – another variation.

4 Larger sheets, with cuts made parallel to the fluting, make cylindrical forms:

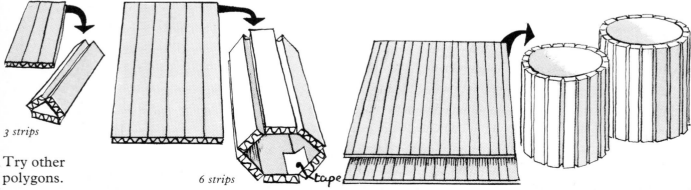

5 Flexible card: to make into a material that can bend and spiral, use the simple corrugated 'paper' or peel off one of the plain layers of Single Wall.

Wet the surface as shown on page 78. If the layer is reluctant to come off, repeat the soaking process or select another type of card.

The result is a surface both decorative and useful for wheel and belt cogs – see page 78 for machines.

6 Finally, corrugated cardboard can of course be used as found – in sheet form. Provided that it is clean and dry (wet card tends to warp), it may be cut into smaller pieces which become the ideal bases for small models. For strong substantial bases, several pieces should be glued together.

To form strong structures without cutting, score or crush the fluting so that it can be folded without breaking. See page 90 for stage scenery. Similarly, long strips of card can be twisted.

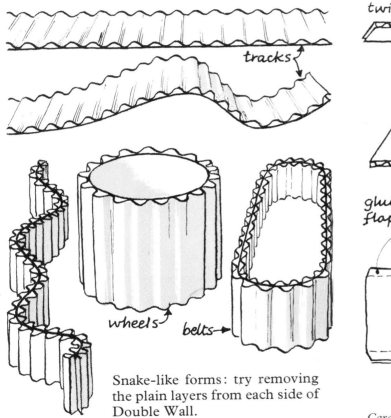

Snake-like forms: try removing the plain layers from each side of Double Wall.

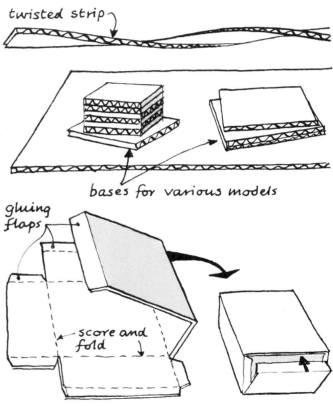

Card crushed and folded across fluting to make strong boxes.

Projects to try

Experiment with this material quickly reveals its versatility. It is ideal both as a craft room material and for stage work. It can be used for sculpture or for the construction of pylons, towers, bridges and buildings. In its flexible form it can be used to make cog and wheel machines and is useful for basic science projects. The following pages are arranged to cover four main groups: sculpture, machines, buildings and stage scenery and props.

SCULPTURE 1

The machine shown on page 68 will prepare a set of strips as shown above, the strips not completely cut through. The length of each strip has still to be decided. The strips used for the constructions shown here and on the following two pages are 15 mm wide by 130 mm long. Experiment with strips of a standard length:

1 Arrange strips fanwise, starting with, say, five or six strips.

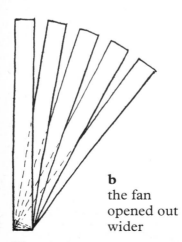

a
each strip
touching and
overlapping
the next

b
the fan
opened out
wider

2 Pivot the strips on a central axis rather than at one end, or between centre and end.

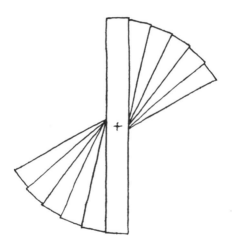

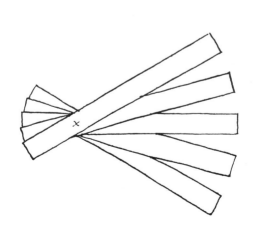

3 Added groups of strips can vary the form:

Five strips
one way,
then back
again . . .

joining
fans
together

Examples of work by 12 and 13 year old children who used strips of a standard length.

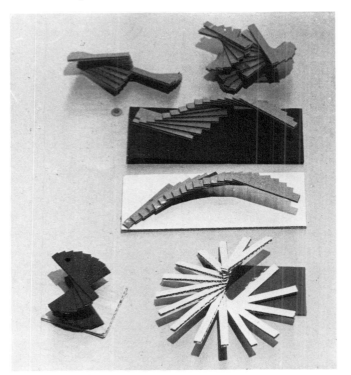

Preparation of materials is essential for successful project work with large groups of young children. Ensure that sufficient strips of card are ready cut — say, twenty for each child — and that small containers of PVA adhesive are available. For smearing on adhesive it is helpful to have a supply of small sticks that can be thrown away after use. Colour may be used as a contrast on some models. Paint bases before gluing constructions on top.

SCULPTURE 2

Use the same width of strip (15 mm) but introduce differing lengths. Try spacing the strips to produce a more linear and curving form.

The illustration below shows one example of this particular type of arrangement. Try many variations on this theme and rearrange the strips in many different ways.

An example of wires supporting strips to create spiral forms. 14 year old.

Also try cutting wedge shapes, of similar or differing length:

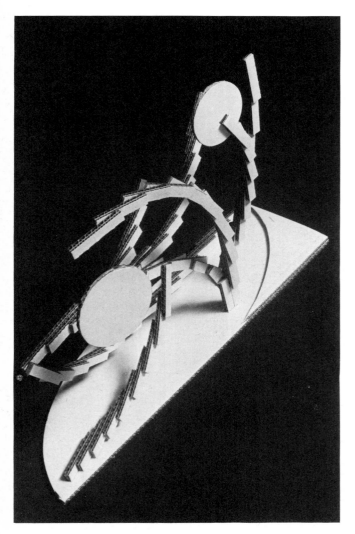

Three-dimensional design based on the circle and curve uses different lengths of strip and incorporates circular pendant pieces threaded to the curves.

Free-standing structure with wedge-shaped pieces. Multi-coloured with emulsion paint. 13 year old.

Spirals and helices

Two examples of the use of different strip lengths are illustrated below. Both designs were based on spiral and helix forms related to a three-sided box. The boxes and strips are all Double-Wall board, glued with PVA adhesive and painted with emulsion paint or sprayed with silver metallic paint.

Note on warping

Larger pieces of board (as used for the box forms shown here) have a tendency to warp and twist if over-painted. To eliminate this problem, paint lightly and thinly and on both sides of the board. Allow to dry thoroughly before gluing structures to the surface.

Below left : three-dimensional design using six spiral (helical) forms. The forms were sprayed with silver and the box was black. 14 year old.

Below : two multi-coloured wing-like forms that touch each other in the central space of the box. 14 year old.

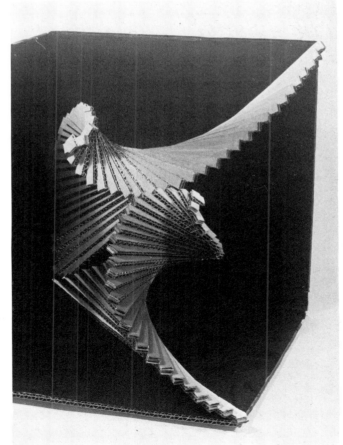

SCULPTURE 3
Twisted forms

If greater lengths of strip are lightly moistened and then twisted round, a spiral (or, more accurately, helical) form can be produced. Held before heat until dry, the strip will retain its new shape. Try building with it. Try also gluing one strip at a right angle to another before moistening and twisting.

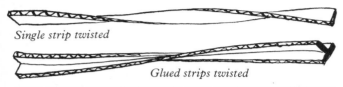

Single strip twisted

Glued strips twisted

A three-dimensional design based on the turning forms of plants. Various lengths and width of single and double pieces have been twisted and glued to a base.

Sculpture on legs

Try building structures that stand on one or more legs on a base of stout card. Start with simple, repeating units and create forms out of more irregular shapes, including wedges, circles, squares, etc.

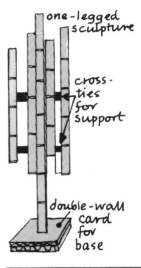

one-legged sculpture

cross-ties for support

double-wall card for base

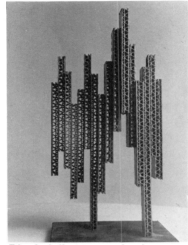

Biped of silver-sprayed strips.

Three-legged structure that uses varying strip lengths.

Naturalistic forms

Animals, birds and fishes can be constructed from a single folded and shaped piece of board. Additional pieces can be glued or slotted onto the first piece. Larger forms can be enhanced by some colouring. Try discarded oddments of spray paint: enamel, metallic and so on.

A hedgehog formed of one basic piece, cut and folded, with spines cut out of the same piece and folded forward.

Basic shape of Single Wall card for hedgehog.

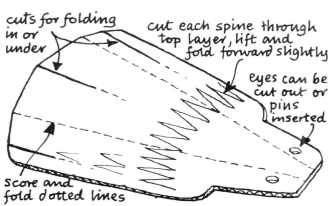

cuts for folding in or under

cut each spine through top layer, lift and fold forward slightly

eyes can be cut out or pins inserted

score and fold dotted lines

Right: two views of a peacock built up from layers of Single Wall card and corrugated paper.

MACHINES 1

The corrugations in this material can be used as cogs on wheels or belts. This property makes it possible to explore a range of mechanically moving parts, both as a pastime and as a means of demonstrating some basic facts of physical science.

It is possible to make wheels, driving belts, tracks and levers from Single Wall card and corrugated paper. The Double Wall card is useful for double-sided tracks if outer layers are removed.

Wheel construction

An essential requirement of any working wheel is that it revolves evenly. To achieve this, it is recommended that you use an accurately centred tin lid. Try collecting the lids of large Sellotape tins or any lids with deep sides.

1 With a pair of compasses, draw a series of concentric rings 2 mm apart on a piece of transparent film or tracing paper:

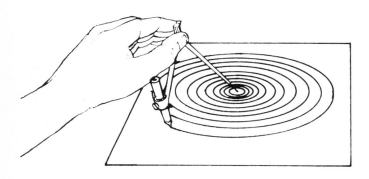

2 Lay on a tin lid. When one of the rings fits the circumference of the tin, mark with a fibre tip pen through centre hole.

tin fitting one of the rings

3 Drill through the centre mark with a drill of a size to suit the proposed axle: thick wire, cane or similar material.

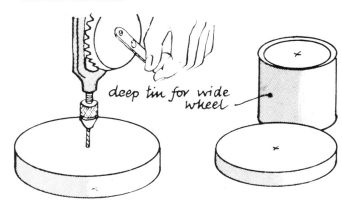

deep tin for wide wheel

4 Prepare card to fit the circumference (+ 25 mm for a tab to glue under) and thickness of the tin lid. Wet one surface of Single Wall card or, on Double Wall card, the two outer layers. Peel off after a minute or two.

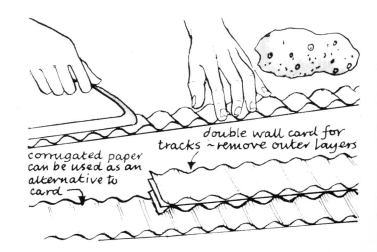

corrugated paper can be used as an alternative to card

double wall card for tracks ~ remove outer layers

5 Place the prepared strip round the tin. If the number of cogs does not fit evenly, stretch slightly, or contract a little, to make it do so.

Mark with a pen the overlapping point, allowing the 25 mm extra for tab.

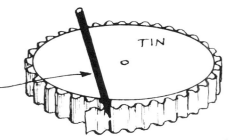

Cut away fluting from tab and glue (**a**), bring other end to the tab and join with small paper clip (**b**) until dry. Glue the edge of the tin lid and draw the 'cog' strip gently over it.

6 For larger and more complex machines a wheel with two axle holes for stability is required.

Try making many different wheels using complete tins with lids, two lids spaced apart as shown below, and lidded plastic containers.

Using two tin lids and a very wide wheel:

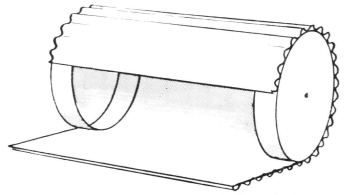

The advantage of using two end pieces is that you can then select your own width of wheel, making it wide enough even to carry several driving belts or wheels, and having maximum stability for the axle.

Experiment using different sizes of wheel on a flat plain surface:

a

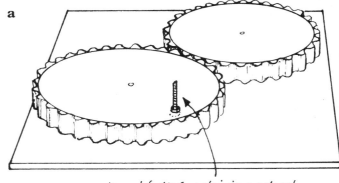

nut and bolt for driving wheel

nail, tack or screw wheels to base

b

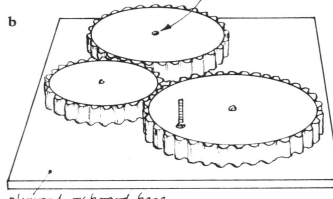

plywood or board base

c

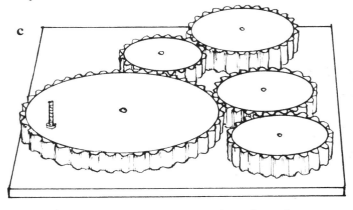

Try a series of experiments to show how forces are transmitted through a driving wheel to other wheels.

MACHINES 2

After experimenting with wheels on their own, try incorporating belts and/or tracks in more elaborate wheel machines.

Belts

1 Driving belts will need to be considerably longer than the strips that make the wheels. Prepare a number of strips as long as possible (in the same manner as for the wheels) allowing 25 mm for tabs – then join together rather more than enough for a belt.

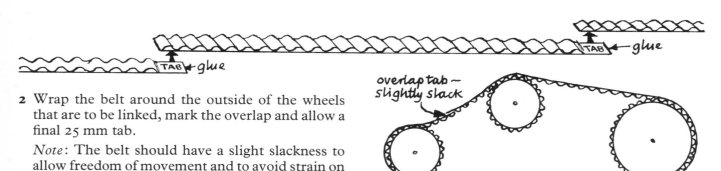

2 Wrap the belt around the outside of the wheels that are to be linked, mark the overlap and allow a final 25 mm tab.

Note: The belt should have a slight slackness to allow freedom of movement and to avoid strain on wheels and axles.

Tracks

Tracks for either running cog wheels or driving wheels should be rigid. Make them from prepared strip (as for belts, above) strengthened on the plain side by a strip glued at a right angle. (Use an impact adhesive for strong bonding.)

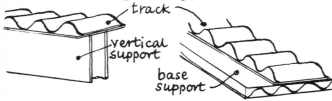

If the track is to be used as a railway, no special support is needed – simply glue to the base board of the machine construction.

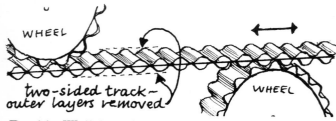

Double Wall board with the outer walls removed will provide a two-sided track or belt. Experiment with wheels on both sides.

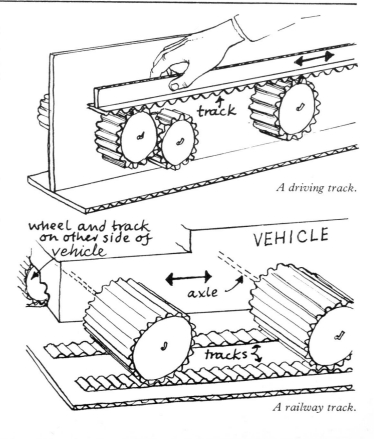

A driving track.

A railway track.

Try experiments using belts with wheels:

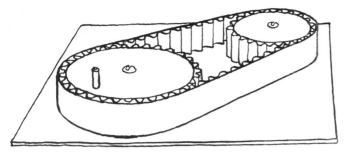

Try wider wheels with two belts, separated by a card disc glued between two sets of 'cogs'.

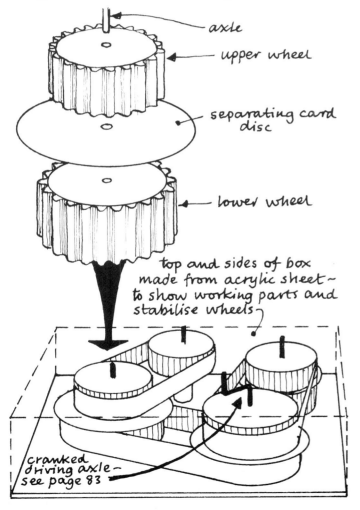

axle

upper wheel

separating card disc

lower wheel

top and sides of box made from acrylic sheet ~ to show working parts and stabilise wheels

cranked driving axle ~ see page 83

Types of driving power

a Simply glue a strip of wood across the side of the tin – or secure with self-tapping screws.

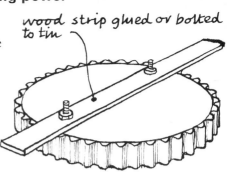

wood strip glued or bolted to tin

Alternatively, drill a hole towards the edge of the tin, fit suitable bolt fitted through a piece of dowelling, tighten and use as a turning handle.

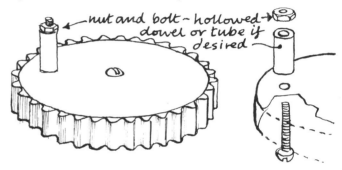

nut and bolt ~ hollowed dowel or tube if desired

b *Motor power*
Try an old clockwork Meccano motor or even a small electric motor suitably geared down.

Elastic drive is suitable for small lightweight models.

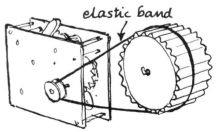

elastic band

Alternatively, fix a cotton reel to the motor, having previously covered it as for a wheel, and make a belt to run from reel to the rest of the machine.

Note: Perfect meshing between cogs should not be expected, especially on small wheels. The larger the wheel (and therefore the number of 'cogs') the better the meshing and smooth running of machine.

MACHINES 3
Supporting structures

Some machines will require not only bases but vertical supports for wheels. These can be of scrap wood or of stiffened corrugated card.

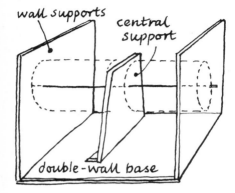

wall supports
central support
double-wall base

Supports can be solid (wood, card or hardboard) or open frame:

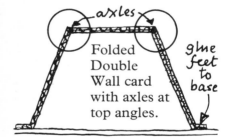

axles

Folded Double Wall card with axles at top angles.

glue feet to base

Holes for axles on all supports must be carefully placed to ensure true turn of wheel.

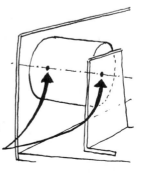

Above and below : two machines using four-sided support structures and plastic drug pots as a basis for wheels. All axles were made from old coat hangers. The belts in these two models were cut direct from a roll of corrugated paper. Both constructed by 13 year olds.

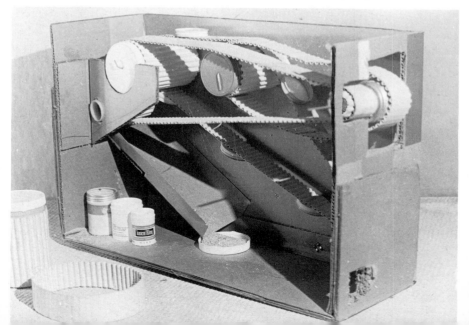

Making a driving wheel

1 Drill centre holes in the lid and base of a tin or pot (see page 78 for method of centring).

2 Drill another hole at one end of the pot, approx. 20 mm from the centre.

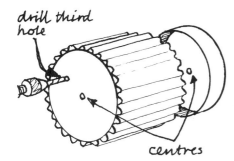

drill third hole

centres

3 Pass axle through centres of lid and base and bend over one end to align with the 3rd hole.

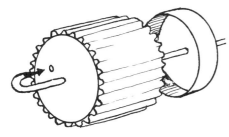

4 Pull the axle rod back through the pot, ensuring that the bent end of axle fits into the 3rd hole. Secure lid.

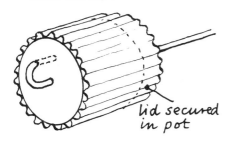

lid secured in pot

5 Pass the straight end of the axle through the support structure of the machine.

6 Bend over the straight end of the axle to form a handle. Wedge it with a piece of rigid material (wood, metal or stiff card) to make the turning action firm without being impossibly stiff.

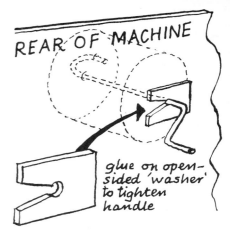

REAR OF MACHINE

glue on open-sided 'washer' to tighten handle

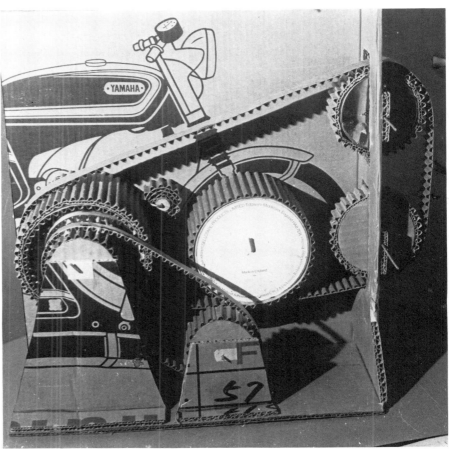

A model that uses four Sellotape tins and part of a motorcycle packing case to make a machine with two belts. Note the double 'gears' on the left-hand wheel.

BUILDINGS 1: Construction methods

Corrugated cardboard can also be considered as a building material for all kinds of models: scale models for architectural schemes (in combination with paper and card or by itself) such as houses, office/flat blocks, town plan layouts, towers, bridges and pylons. The material can similarly be used in geographical or science projects.

Towers, pylons and bridges

Such tall constructions are dependent on a grid framework made from strips of corrugated card:

a glue diagonal strips into corners

cut out halving joints and glue together

b If structures are very high, make stronger vertical and horizontal members.

strip glued to side to make 'T' section

cut one layer and fold

With these basic building units, many towers and bridges can be developed.

Suspension bridge

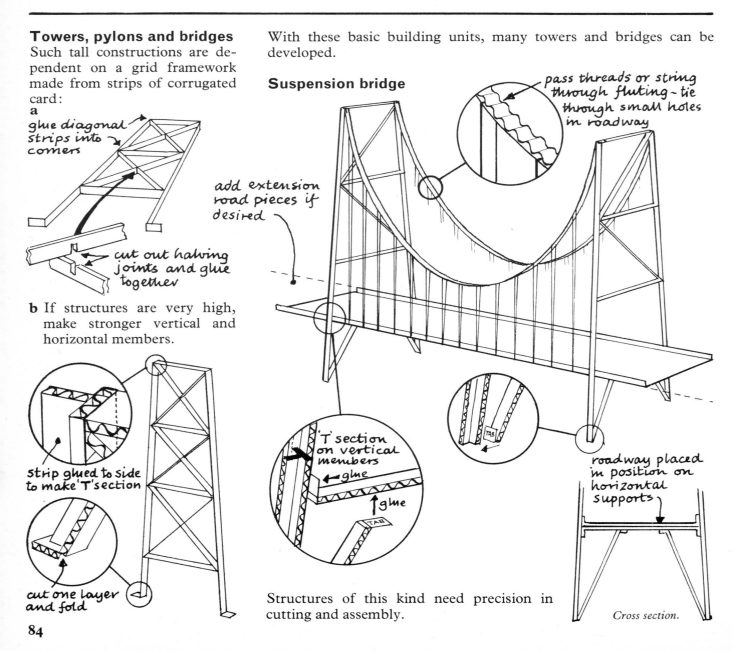

pass threads or string through fluting - tie through small holes in roadway

add extension road pieces if desired

'T' section on vertical members — glue

glue

roadway placed in position on horizontal supports

Cross section.

Structures of this kind need precision in cutting and assembly.

To make tall pylons and towers
Prepare a scale drawing for one side. Lay the cut strips of card over the drawing and lightly glue with an impact adhesive (Evo-Stik in U.K.). Repeat up to the number of sides required for square or other polygonal structures.

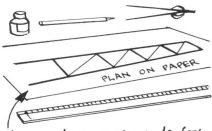

drawn plan – use a rule for accurate dimensions

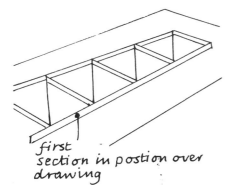

first section in postion over drawing

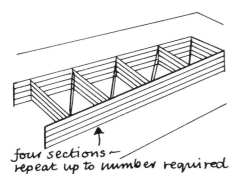

four sections – repeat up to number required

A group of pylons built on a grid system. Note the variety of form within the basic grid structure. A useful starting point for group work is the study of telecommunication towers in different parts of the country.

BUILDINGS 2: Tower blocks, cities, towns

In addition to open-frame forms, towers can be made from sets of joined strips folded to suit requirements. Take a sheet of Single Wall card cut into strips only down to the further plain layer (see page 70).

Sets of three, four or more strips can be cut off the sheet, folded into 'solids' and joined with adhesive tape inside.

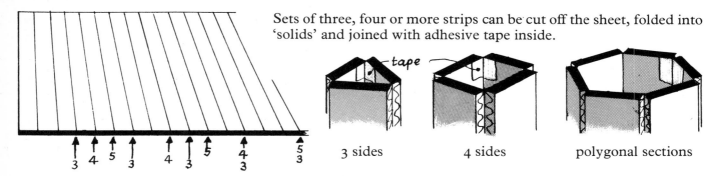

3 sides   4 sides   polygonal sections

The illustration on the right shows the use to which box structures can be put. A city of skyscrapers and lower apartment blocks.

If the boxes are made in a wide range of sizes and can be fitted one inside another a more interesting silhouette will result.

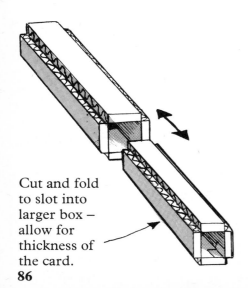

Cut and fold to slot into larger box — allow for thickness of the card.

Cylindrical/polygonal forms

Spiralling towers can be built from separate pieces of identical shape:

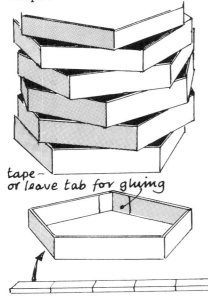

tape — or leave tab for gluing

A set of twelve strips cut as a unit from the sheet can be joined to make a round tower:

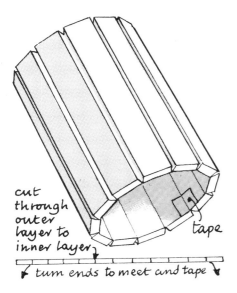

cut through outer layer to inner layer

tape

turn ends to meet and tape

Two examples of tower structures: note the round tower above and the dome-like structure below — both employed the cutting method shown in the drawing bottom left. Both models were made by 13 year old children.

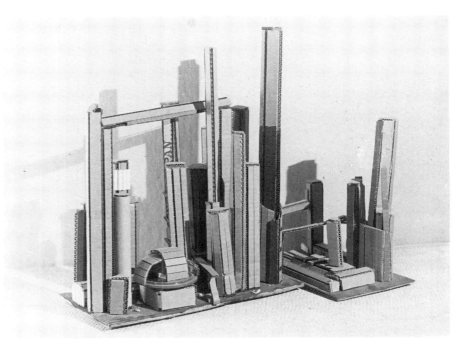

BUILDINGS 3: Layered walling

Try building walls with Double Wall strips. Glue twelve strips one above another in layers. Use PVA adhesive diluted 1:1 with water and grip the layers together with small paper clips while the adhesive dries. This will make a strong wall and save time.

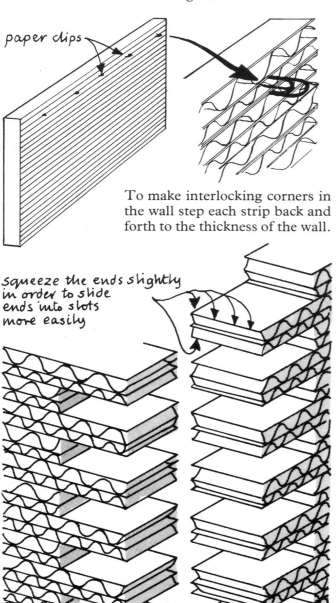

paper clips

To make interlocking corners in the wall step each strip back and forth to the thickness of the wall.

squeeze the ends slightly in order to slide ends into slots more easily

When the card has been cut at a right angle to the fluting, a wall of it has an open mesh pattern that appears rather transparent. This can be used to effect if you also explore lighting techniques.

As an alternative texture, try cutting the card at a variety of angles to the fluting. The appearance will be more or less opaque. Try alternating the layers in the wall for greater textural effect.

fluting
45° cutting

Appearance of cut strips:

a

b

c

The length of wave is determined by the cutting angle: **a** has fluting cut at a right angle; **b** at 40°; **c** at 50°.

Alternating layers will vary the texture of the wall:

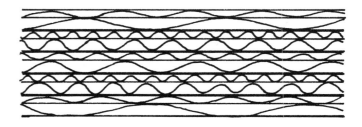

Try also leaving gaps in every second layer:

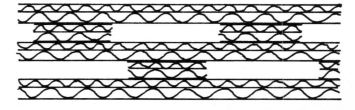

Doors and windows

Windows and doors must be considered before the walls are glued. In the example shown on the right, the door opening has been made by using shorter strips to build the wall each side up the height of the door.

Window openings are made in the same way.

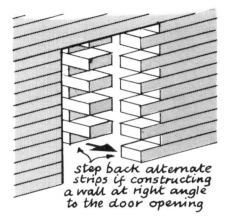

step back alternate strips if constructing a wall at right angle to the door opening

Stairs

Cut strips to the required number of steps, each strip being shorter by the depth of a stair tread:

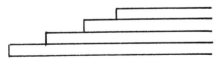

Open-plan stairs – cut equal pieces of card as shown:

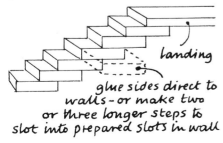

landing

glue sides direct to walls – or make two or three longer steps to slot into prepared slots in wall

An example of layered walling with strips cut at a right angle to the fluting. The completed wall sections are being brought into contact.

Roofs

Roofs can be flat, lean-to or pitched. Flat roofs can be glued directly to the tops of walls.

Pitched roofs are scored and folded (centrally or to one side as required) with end pieces cut and glued into position before roofs are fixed to walls.

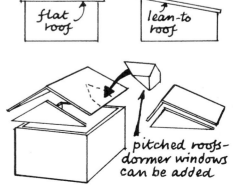

flat roof

lean-to roof

pitched roofs – dormer windows can be added

89

STAGE SCENERY AND PROPERTIES 1

Drama productions can benefit financially from the use of cardboard. It does, of course, have disadvantages – it is easily crushed and bent – but it can be used in areas least likely to be knocked or pushed against. Structures of considerable height and breadth can be built with Double or Triple Wall card but they must be well sprayed with an appropriate fire-proofing solution.

The setting illustrated on these two pages was for a one-act play by Ray Bradbury called 'Pillar of Fire'. The text demanded two basic elements – a tomb and a futuristic incinerator for the disposal of various characters!

Very quick scene changes were necessary. This was achieved by designing the incinerator to interlock with the tomb which was a set-piece on stage.

Basic design
It is useful to make models in paper or thin card (say, a scale of 4 cm to 1 m) before attempting to cut out actual settings. This will ensure that all folding and cutting will be accurate.

In this case an equilateral triangle was taken as the basic shape. This was built up with three pieces of Double Wall motorcycle packing case cut to an identical shape.

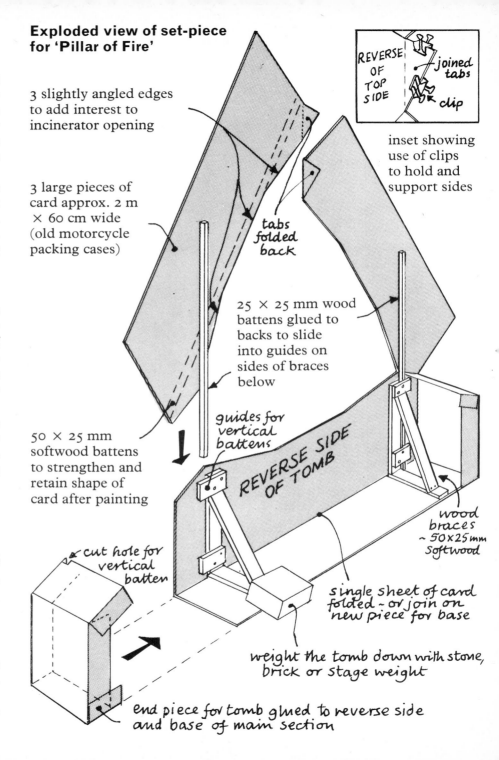

Exploded view of set-piece for 'Pillar of Fire'

3 slightly angled edges to add interest to incinerator opening

3 large pieces of card approx. 2 m × 60 cm wide (old motorcycle packing cases)

50 × 25 mm softwood battens to strengthen and retain shape of card after painting

tabs folded back

25 × 25 mm wood battens glued to backs to slide into guides on sides of braces below

guides for vertical battens

REVERSE SIDE OF TOMB

REVERSE OF TOP SIDE · joined tabs · clip

inset showing use of clips to hold and support sides

wood braces ~ 50×25mm softwood

cut hole for vertical batten

single sheet of card folded - or join on new piece for base

weight the tomb down with stone, brick or stage weight

end piece for tomb glued to reverse side and base of main section

Rear of tomb: use one of the upper pieces if required.

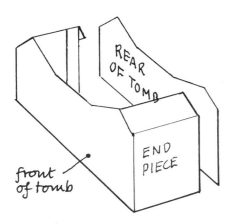

If the tomb position is back centre of the stage, a backing will not be necessary. However, placing the tomb to the left or right of the stage will reveal its two-dimensional shape and a backing will be required – use one of the two upper pieces and arrange the attached batten to project behind a curtain.

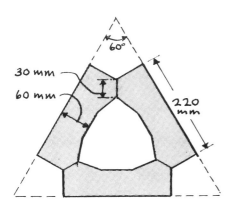

Diagram of shape with dimensions.

Assembling the incinerator sides on top of the tomb in the workshop. Note the use of scrap metal pieces on inner edges.

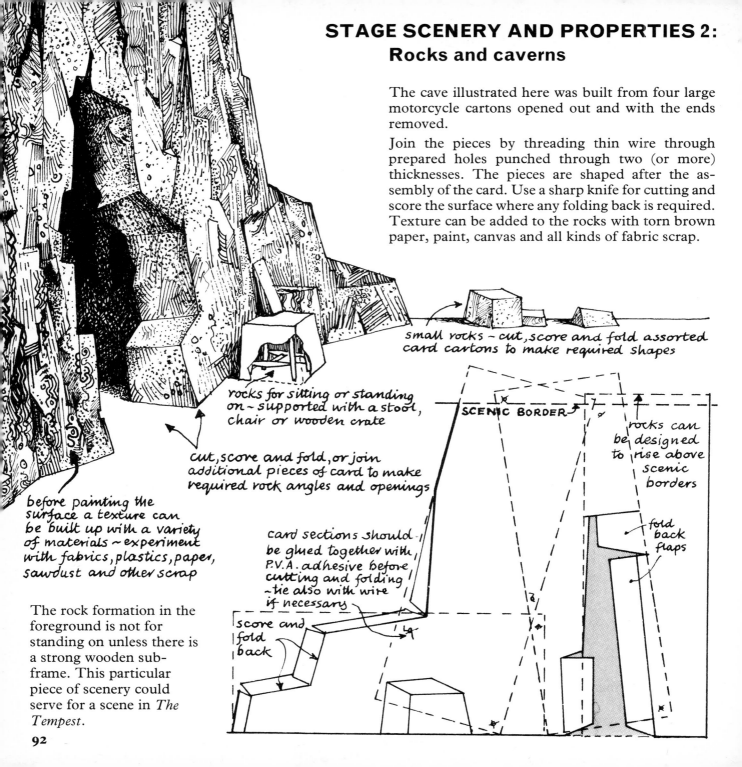

STAGE SCENERY AND PROPERTIES 2:
Rocks and caverns

The cave illustrated here was built from four large motorcycle cartons opened out and with the ends removed.

Join the pieces by threading thin wire through prepared holes punched through two (or more) thicknesses. The pieces are shaped after the assembly of the card. Use a sharp knife for cutting and score the surface where any folding back is required. Texture can be added to the rocks with torn brown paper, paint, canvas and all kinds of fabric scrap.

small rocks ~ cut, score and fold assorted card cartons to make required shapes

rocks for sitting or standing on ~ supported with a stool, chair or wooden crate

SCENIC BORDER

rocks can be designed to rise above scenic borders

cut, score and fold, or join additional pieces of card to make required rock angles and openings

fold back flaps

before painting the surface a texture can be built up with a variety of materials ~ experiment with fabrics, plastics, paper, sawdust and other scrap

card sections should be glued together with P.V.A. adhesive before cutting and folding ~ tie also with wire if necessary

score and fold back

The rock formation in the foreground is not for standing on unless there is a strong wooden sub-frame. This particular piece of scenery could serve for a scene in *The Tempest*.

Displays at fairs or festivals

Corrugated Double Wall cardboard is an ideal material for any kind of display at May and Summer fairs. It can be used to face stalls, stands or, in this example, an outdoor theatre. This was designed in the style of a Dutch organ with a large opening for a small school choir and a band. It was constructed round a metal frame and used old pieces of wood batten from a building site and a sawmill. The whole surface of card, front and behind, may be painted with emulsion paint to make it waterproof. This will preserve it against damp or wet conditions and preserve it for future use. Other projects – puppet stands, Punch and Judy theatres and so on – can also be attempted with corrugated cardboard.

Rear view of theatre – note the slotted metal-angle step frame and the wood framing.

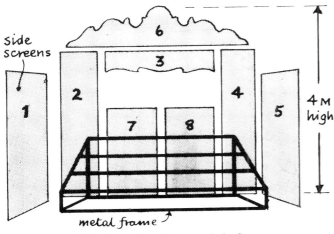

Eight pieces of card surround the frame.

The 'Dutch' organ near completion – built from refrigerator and motorcycle packing cartons.

STAGE SCENERY AND PROPERTIES 3: Armour

Corrugated paper (i.e. one single plain layer + fluting) is useful for arm and leg armour, if a great amount is needed for a particular stage production. For it is necessary first to make a dummy of softwood on which to mould the cardboard. This material is not suitable for breast armour unless it can be of a very crude type. The flat brims of some helmets can be fashioned from it and other small items.

Making and using a dummy
Join three pieces of softwood by gluing and screwing, then shape to this section:

Cover the dummy with greaseproof paper. Lay over it first a layer of corrugated paper with the fluting upward and then, after gluing, lay another layer of glued 'paper' with the fluting downward into the first layer. Work the two layers together.

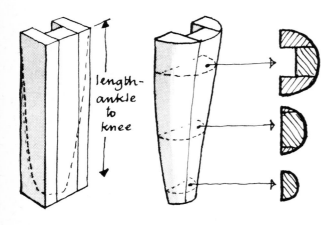

length-
ankle
to
knee

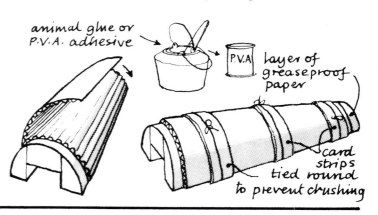

animal glue or
P.V.A. adhesive

P.V.A

layer of
greaseproof
paper

card
strips
tied round
to prevent crushing

Leg armour (greaves)
Remove the 'paper' mouldings from the dummy when dry. Cut into shape and decorate.

Arm armour
The upper and lower arms can be covered by straight near-cylinders of cardboard made similarly to the greaves. The joints are of cardboard strips fastened to each other and to the upper and lower arm pieces with long paper fasteners that allow the joints to work.

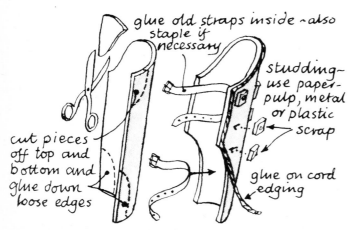

glue old straps inside ~also
staple if
necessary

studding-
use paper-
pulp, metal
or plastic
scrap

cut pieces
off top and
bottom and
glue down
loose edges

glue on cord
edging

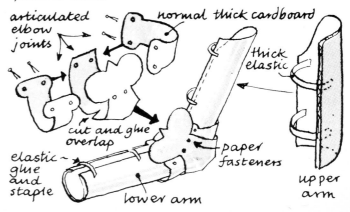

articulated
elbow
joints

normal thick cardboard

thick
elastic

cut and glue
overlap

elastic~
glue
and
staple

paper
fasteners

lower arm

upper
arm

Buckets and boxes

Corrugated card is particularly suitable for wooden slatted objects: pails, buckets, bins or large bowls. The slatted effect is achieved by cutting through the fluting at intervals of approx. 50 mm (these cuts need not be too regular). A realistic finish can be given by covering with brown/ochre paint.

The large bucket illustrated here was constructed of Single Wall card round a large metal container which had held honey. The 'straps' are of silvery plastic bands from large packing cartons – another material from the scrap heap.

Also comparatively simple to make are boxes and caskets. Cut carefully and join the edges with PVA or impact adhesive; alternatively, tape all edges with brown sticky tape.

The lid is cut after the completion of gluing. Mark carefully with a rule to the desired depth of lid and cut through on three sides. Score and fold the fourth (hinged) side. Fix clip devices if preferred.

Decorate with any scrap objects such as beads, washers or seeds, and/or with metal paint or lacquer. Handles can be of wire simply pushed through the card.

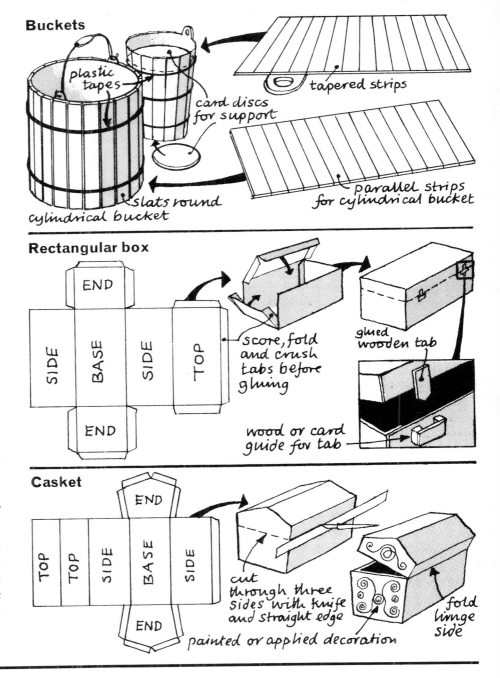

Buckets

plastic tapes

tapered strips

card discs for support

parallel strips for cylindrical bucket

slats round cylindrical bucket

Rectangular box

END · SIDE · BASE · SIDE · TOP · END

score, fold and crush tabs before gluing

glued wooden tab

wood or card guide for tab

Casket

END · TOP · TOP · SIDE · BASE · SIDE · END

cut through three sides with knife and straight edge

painted or applied decoration

fold hinge side

Furniture

It is important to reckon how much wear the items are likely to receive, but it is usually more satisfactory (and easier) to construct furniture over a timber framework than to build entirely with card.

MAP MODELLING

There are various methods of map modelling. This example is a map in relief showing 50 ft contours.

Corrugated card does have a useful advantage for this purpose – correct scale thickness in a material that is easy to cut. Use the Double Wall card, allowing one thickness to 50 ft.

Select from a large-scale map a small area that has well-spaced contours:

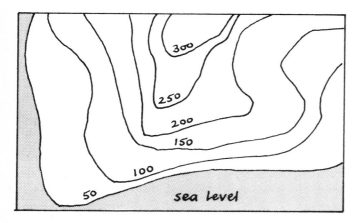

With one layer of card to 50 ft, there are six layers to take the contours from sea level to 300 ft.

Layer method

1 Trace the contours and transfer one to each separate sheet of card + the next higher contour. Cut around the outer contour and use the inner as a guide when gluing on the next piece.

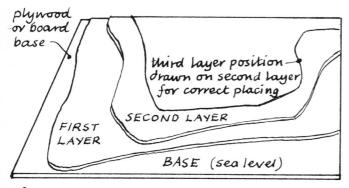

2 Proceed through the layers from largest to smallest which will be the highest point.

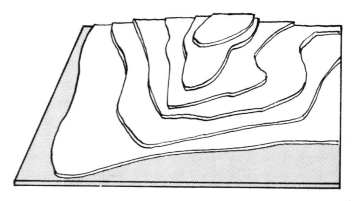

Note: If water is part of the model, an old mirror can serve as a base. Metal foil is an alternative. For small lakes or pools a broken hand mirror will do.

3 *Filling in*. The filling-in material must be comparatively soft so that it can be moulded into a smooth surface for the relief map (corrugated card will not take much pressure). Plaster of Paris is suitable. Very pliable paper pulp can be used if the card is first coated with a waterproof layer – varnish or paint. See page 59 for pulp making.

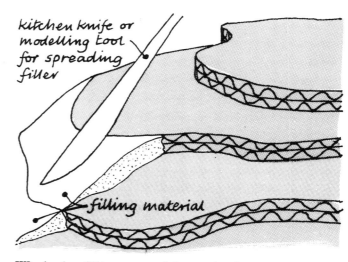

Work the filling material evenly from the leading edge of each contour level *up* to the next leading edge.

Metal

4

1 tin cans; 2 coat hangers; 3 stampings; 4 TV tubing and assorted tubes; 5 rods and bicycle spokes; 6 angle and strip metal; 7 nails, screws and washers; 8 wire, 9 metal gauze; 10 gauze and perforated sheet; 11 foil and sheet metal; 12 swarf and springs

SCRAP METAL

The variety of interesting design projects and sculptures from used tin-cans, metal coat-hangers, bicycle spokes and other metal scrap is potentially endless. The fascinating shapes and forms found in a scrap metal yard offer a wide range of possibilities for experiment and innovation – for a few pence.

The ideas suggested or described here for the use of scrap metal require only simple basic skills. Well-known techniques for soldering and brazing, for example, are mentioned, but further information on these and other techniques should be sought from specialist books.

The basic forms are: sheet, bar, rod, wire, strip, wire mesh ('chicken wire'), fabric (woven wire), perforated, moulded and stamped sheet.

Properties and descriptions of metals

Properties

MALLEABILITY: Can be hammered without cracking, and shaped by pressure. The thicker the metal, the less malleable.

DUCTILITY: Can be stretched or hammered without tearing.

DENSITY: Relationship of weight to size – the greater the weight to a particular size, the denser the metal.

SOLDERABILITY: The ability of a metal to be joined to another or to itself by means of soft solder or brazing.

Description of metals most frequently found as scrap

COPPER: A reddish metal, solderable.

BRASS: A yellow-red metal, less malleable than copper. Requires annealing (heating) when worked. Solderable.

ALUMINIUM: Silver-grey, malleable and ductile. Will not tarnish. Not solderable – must be riveted, or joined with epoxy resin adhesives. Found in many forms: foil, sheet, wire and rod.

MILD STEEL: e.g. in wrought iron, wire and some nails. Greyish in colour, solderable if resin flux used.

ZINC: When old, a very soft dull grey – frequently in perforated sheet form. Solderable with cored solder or any soft-soldering method.

Sources of supply

Always contact managers or foremen in the first instance.

SCRAP YARDS: All kinds of forms of metal at scrap prices.

INDUSTRY: Engineering works and garages can sometimes supply scrap. Sheet metal works often punch out aluminium sheet leaving a large quantity of discs as scrap (studding). The waste from lathe-turning (swarf) is also useful.

IRONMONGERY AND HARDWARE: Wholesalers will occasionally supply 'sweepings' (bags of assorted nails, screws, washers, etc.) for a few pence.

FARMS AND BUILDING SITES: Wire mesh ('chicken wire') oddments.

THE HOME: Foil, pie-cases, coat-hangers, tin cans, tin tacks, etc.

TOOLS

1 Saws for thick sheet and rod. Piercing saw for fine work.

2 Assorted sheet metal cutters
   a shears for thick sheet
   b snips for thin sheet
   c scissors for foil

3 Wire cutters: electrical for very fine wire; standard for medium gauge wire; heavy-duty for heavy gauge wire.

4 Pliers for holding and shaping: round nose for curling; flat nose for angles; adjustable for holding and bending heavy-gauge wire and nails.

5 Hammers: ball-pein or cross-pein for general work, beating and flattening; tack hammer for delicate work; round-headed wooden mallet for hammering the surface of thin metal sheet (to form shallow dishes, etc.)

6 Various holding tools: vices for bench work; hand vice and 'G' clamps for light work.

7 Drills and punches: hand or electric drills for soft metals; special plier punch for harder work (not essential); nail punches.

8 Files for smoothing rough surfaces and edges, also for cutting lines in decorative work.

9 Irons and torches for soldering; torch for large or faster work.

10 Rivets, riveting pliers and adhesives for metals that cannot be soldered.

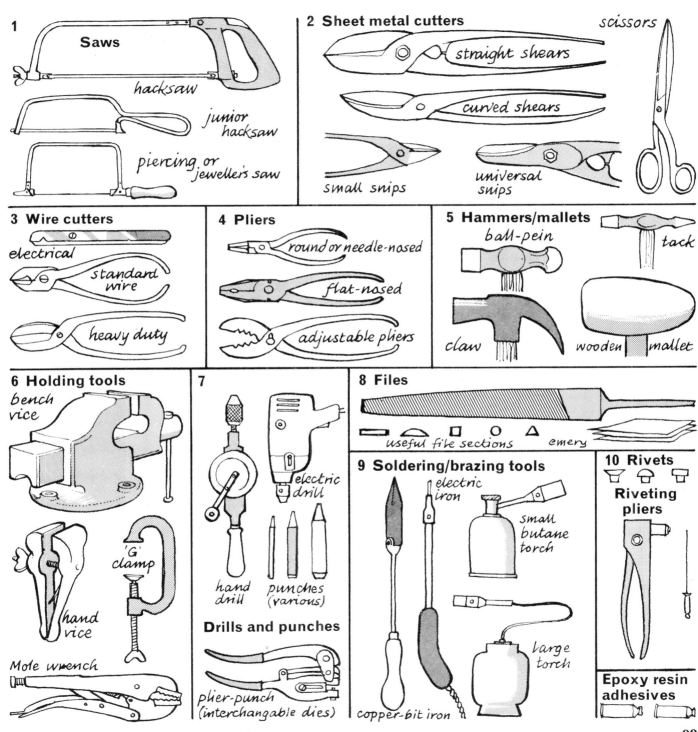

1 Saws
hacksaw
junior hacksaw
piercing or jeweller's saw

2 Sheet metal cutters
straight shears
curved shears
small snips
universal snips
scissors

3 Wire cutters
electrical
standard wire
heavy duty

4 Pliers
round or needle-nosed
flat-nosed
adjustable pliers

5 Hammers/mallets
ball-pein
tack
claw
wooden mallet

6 Holding tools
bench vice
'G' clamp
hand vice
Mole wrench

7
electric drill
hand drill
punches (various)

Drills and punches
plier-punch (interchangable dies)

8 Files
useful file sections
emery

9 Soldering/brazing tools
electric iron
small butane torch
large torch
copper-bit iron

10 Rivets
Riveting pliers

Epoxy resin adhesives

WIRE: Bending, twisting and hammering

Wire may come in a wide assortment of thickness, hardness or softness (malleability and ductility), and colour. Very thin binding wires 0·6 mm thick or less, and wires wrapped within small electrical motors, are fairly plentiful in odd corners of workshops and waste metal dumps. Thicker gauges of soft wire 1 mm thick in aluminium or copper can be acquired for a few pence from scrap metal merchants or from a local firm that discards wire as waste. Galvanised steel wire from 1·2 mm thick up to 12 gauge can often be found on dumps or in garages or farmyards. Bicycle spokes are sometimes available from old wheels – the shine can soon be restored by the use of emery paper.

Bending aluminium wire

Soft aluminium wire 1 mm thick or oddments of wire from an old telephone cable are ideal for use by beginners. Young fingers will find such wire easy to control and quick results will give considerable enjoyment. Try a series of 'waves' between imaginary parallel lines:

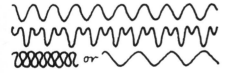

The repetition of one or more of these line patterns can make a variety of all-over designs:

These and similar designs can be mounted on card or joined with fine wire to form pendants, etc.

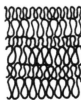

Another interesting shape is the spiral:

Try as many variations as possible and then develop one into a finished design.

Examples of a project with 12 year olds. Twelve to fifteen spiral forms were arranged in various patterns. One represented a wig or hairstyle. Another (bottom left) aimed at a gradual opening of the spiral.

Bending stiff wire

Thicker or harder wire is difficult to form by hand and requires the use of pliers. Tight close curls can be made on the points of round-nosed pliers, larger curves made with less pressure on the lower end of the same pliers:

small curves

larger curls

Wide, long curves are best formed by hand or by pulling over the edge of a table or bench:

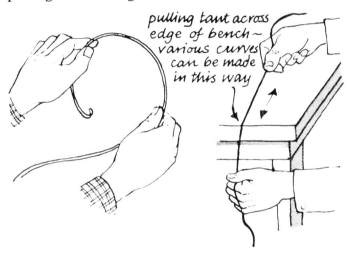

pulling taut across edge of bench ~ various curves can be made in this way

Angles can be formed in wire between the jaws of flat-nose pliers by bending while the wire is being pulled. Repeated angles can be achieved in this way. Very thick or tough wire can more easily be bent in the jaws of a metal worker's vice:

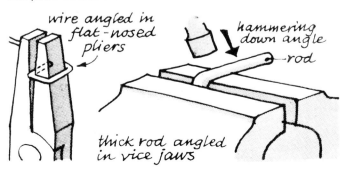

wire angled in flat-nosed pliers

hammering down angle ~ rod

thick rod angled in vice jaws

Bending on a jig

If a pattern of repeated loops, say for a piece of jewellery, is required, some simple jigs can be constructed:

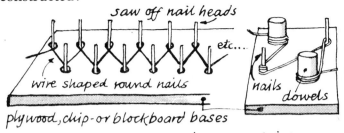

saw off nail heads

etc....

wire shaped round nails

nails dowels

plywood, chip- or blockboard bases

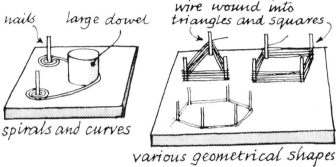

nails

large dowel

wire wound into triangles and squares

spirals and curves

various geometrical shapes

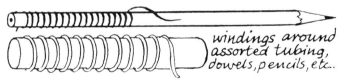

windings around assorted tubing, dowels, pencils, etc..

Repeated forms in wire can be joined with fine wire, soldered or interlocked to make decorative patterns or pieces of jewellery:

a series of loops using a jig ~ see top left

ties

Examples of jewellery and other forms made from metal that includes wire are described and illustrated on page 125.

Rod and thick wire

Any wire that is 12 gauge or over is called a rod. Such thick, hard wire lends itself to standing structures and can be joined by soldering (described on page 118), by tying with fine binding wire or, occasionally, by the use of epoxy resin adhesive.

The two tree forms below are worked with two types of wire, one hard and one soft. The tree on the left is constructed from bicycle spokes which are rigid and hard to bend – whereas the right-hand tree is made from easy-to-bend assorted aluminium wire.

Bicycle-spoke tree : the nature of the hard steel is reflected in the form of the design. 14 year old.

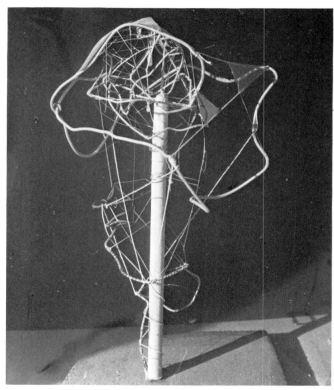

A soft aluminium wire tree (using a wide range of gauge) allows a twisting, contorted form because of the easy bending. 15 year old.

Hammered patterns

Soft wire – copper, aluminium or alloys of aluminium with tin or zinc – can be hammered over a metal base to give many attractive patterns. Place the wire on a bench anvil or steel plate and strike with the flat face of a hammer. Try hitting the wire at regular intervals: first in the centre of each length, then of each half length and so on, alternating from one side of the first centre to the other. Controlled hammering can be achieved with a wide-ended nail punch.

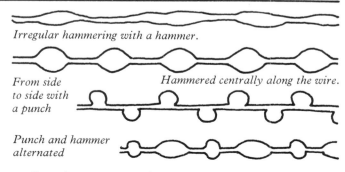

Irregular hammering with a hammer.

From side to side with a punch

Hammered centrally along the wire.

Punch and hammer alternated

See also page 125 for another use of hammering.

Rods combined with metal oddments

Straight steel or brass wire can usefully be combined with other metal scrap to build abstract constructions in three dimensions. Wire that bends too easily (aluminium and copper) is not suitable. Odd lengths of rod and wire (bicycle spokes, for example) lend themselves.

Select about six pieces and decide upon the type of structure you wish to build. The two examples illustrated here started as ideas based on the circle and square. Alternatives could be triangles, rings, flower petals and many other shapes.

The circular metal shapes shown here were pieces of brass stamped out of a sheet and two larger steel discs. The vertical supports were linked to a curved base cut from a large tin can. The square design was built up from pieces of tin and mild steel.

Each construction was soldered with soft solder. First cover each surface with solder (this is called tinning) and then place two surfaces together and heat until they melt together. An additional touch of solder to the tinned parts will ensure a strong joint. Alternatively, epoxy resin adhesive could be used to join metals together.

Experiment with various scrap pieces of metal and curved wire supports.

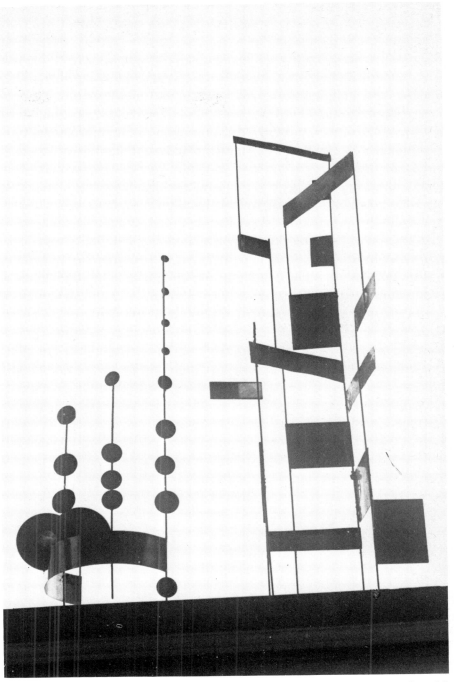

Two constructions using wire and rod : bicycle spokes and brass wire oddments together with assorted oddments of brass, tin and mild steel.

103

SHEET METAL

A wide range of thicknesses and forms of sheet metal are available as scrap; aluminium and tin alloys, copper and steels are to be had for a few pence from most scrap merchants. Local light industry may be able to supply such scrap – it is usually better to make personal contact and to state if you work with youth groups.

Strips of steel are unworkable for young children but may prove useful as bases for mounting work. Soft metal sheet (aluminium, tin, copper and the various alloys) is a versatile material. It can be cut, bent, curled, incised with sharp points and embossed with a hammer and punch. Such a range of techniques allows a wide variety of projects in craftwork.

A useful first exercise for young fingers is the cutting of a square of metal 100 × 100 mm with a pair of tin snips in order to make an interesting design. Give each child in the group the same basic shape and see how many transformations can be achieved – see the illustration below.

From such simple and basic exercises techniques can be learnt and then applied to larger surface areas. See also the section on tin cans (page 120).

Nine different forms from the basic square made by young children as a first exercise. They allow an exploration of metal cutting techniques. One of the original squares of metal is shown bottom left.

Sheet metal projects

The following themes, and many more, suggest themselves as starting points for design ideas: the ebb and flow of waves; water movements in river, stream, lake and waterfall; fire, smoke and flame; wind and the associated swirling movements of leaves.

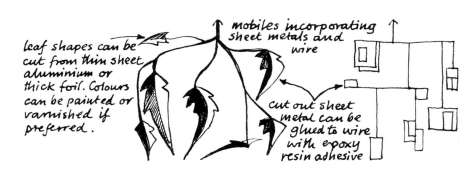

leaf shapes can be cut from thin sheet aluminium or thick foil. Colours can be painted or varnished if preferred.

mobiles incorporating sheet metals and wire

cut out sheet metal can be glued to wire with epoxy resin adhesive

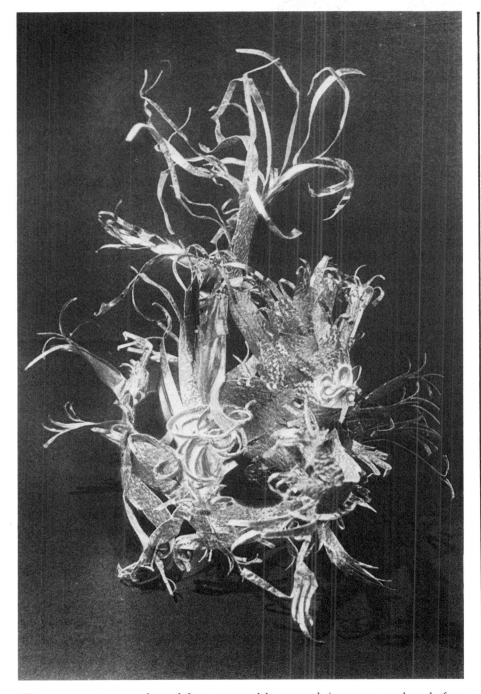

Wave movements: a sculptural form suggested by research into waves and made from embossed sheet aluminium alloy. Made by 14 year old.

METAL FOIL 1

Foil, a thin metal sheet of aluminium or, more rarely, copper is a shiny reflective material. Scrap metal foil is available from a number of sources and in a number of thicknesses:

Very thin: sweet wrappers and many forms of decorations, often in metallic colours.

Thin: oddments of standard kitchen foil and some kitchen wrapping (coloured).

Medium: discarded pie cases and similar food containers often associated with deep freezers. Occasionally flat offcuts from a scrap merchant.

Thick: old lithographic printing plates sometimes obtainable from local printers or a scrap merchant. These come in two thicknesses.

Tools and equipment

Scissors for cutting foil.

A set of modelling tools home made from wood pieces or spoon handles, or boxwood modelling tools as used in clay work.

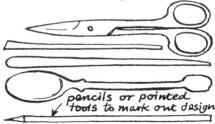

pencils or pointed tools to mark out design

A suitable working base of a thick pile of newspaper or a thick sheet of rubber. Rubber is better but either kind should be soft enough to give under pressure.

105

METAL FOIL 2: Relief

Foil relief is a method of tooling or 'repoussage' where parts of a design are embossed by applying pressure with a modelling tool on the reverse side in order to raise parts of the design from the flat background.

1 Draw a design on a piece of thin paper, keeping it free of small details (something suggestive of a continuous flowing line of hills with the contours of fields, etc. would be suitable). Cut a piece of foil with scissors to the same size as the paper – about 100 × 150 mm will be large enough for a first attempt. Place the foil on the working base of newspaper or rubber with the paper on top. Tape down the corners.

2 Draw over the lines of the design with a ballpoint pen or hard pencil with sufficient pressure to impress a line into the foil. Lift one corner of the paper to see that a clear line is visible. When you have finished, remove the original drawing and lightly reinforce the lines on the foil.

3 Consider which parts of the design should be raised from the flat background and which should recede into it. Note this on your drawing by writing 'up' and 'down' in the relevant areas.

4 Turn over the marked piece of foil on the base pad. Draw a careful line with a pointed tool just within each 'up' area. (Check with your drawing and remember that all shapes are back to front when the foil is this way up.)

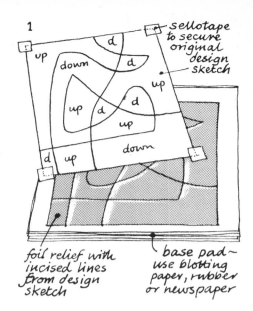

1

sellotape to secure original design sketch

foil relief with incised lines from design sketch

base pad – use blotting paper, rubber or newspaper

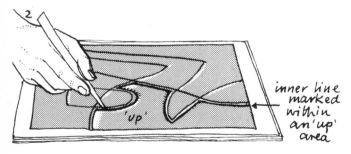

2

inner line marked within an 'up' area

5 Turn the foil again to the 'front' side. With a smooth blunt tool rub carefully all 'down' areas up to the original outlines.

6 Turn the foil yet again and rub all the 'up' areas.

Continue turning and rubbing the foil until you achieve the depth of relief required.

7 The 'up' and 'down' areas can now be textured with a variety of marks and patterns or left plain. Experiment with all your modelling tools on oddments of scrap foil before working on your final relief.

Pattern and texture

Try using a wide range of dot and line patterns on the raised and receded areas. At the same time consider the value of contrast by leaving some areas plain against the patterned textures. Imagine your relief as a kind of landscape with ploughed fields, clusters of trees, patterns of hay bales, smooth water or meadowland. Try to achieve variety in the textures you make.

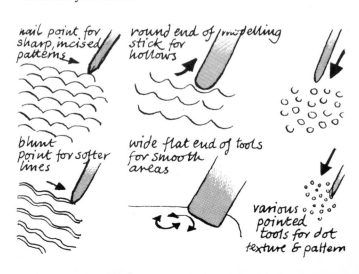

nail point for sharp, incised patterns

round end of modelling stick for hollows

blunt point for softer lines

wide flat end of tools for smooth areas

various pointed tools for dot texture & pattern

A 'landscape' of pattern and texture.

Other projects for reliefs
For relief work with groups of children try ideas based on natural forms (fish, birds, landscape), on sculptural relief (medallions, friezes, relief sculptures), on circular forms (sunbursts, rosettes, flowers), on Christmas decorations, on heraldic devices . . .

Demon head.

Examples of foil relief work from school and youth club.

A surface treatment has been used on some examples. Scour the surface gently with wire wool and soap to remove any grease and the high finish. Rub in Indian ink with a piece of cotton cloth or brush on black varnish. Take ink or varnish across the surface in one direction only. If this does not 'take' spread across in another direction. Any stubborn bits of surface can be removed with sand or emery paper. If you are fortunate enough to have made a copper foil relief, try applying heat with a soldering torch moved rapidly over the surface.

Fish. Note the use of textures and patterns shown in sketch on opposite page.

METAL FOIL 3:
Deep relief

Coloured metal foils can be used in another way to give the appearance of relief work if they are glued to a prepared card or paper base.

In the example shown on the left foils were built up round a central twisted form to convey the feeling of water falling from a pipe and splashing onto a flat surface. This design was created as a display to suggest ideas for creative movement in drama classes and, at the same time, was used to explore the potential in metal foil techniques. This type of subject can be extended to a wider range of natural movement: waterfalls, plant growth, whirlwinds, and so on.

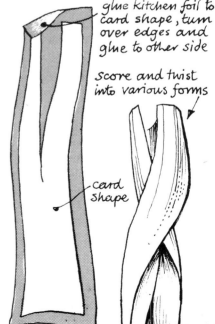

glue kitchen foil to card shape, turn over edges and glue to other side

score and twist into various forms

card shape

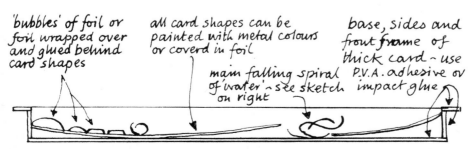

'bubbles' of foil or foil wrapped over and glued behind card shapes

all card shapes can be painted with metal colours or coverd in foil

base, sides and front frame of thick card - use P.V.A. adhesive or impact glue

main falling spiral of 'water' - see sketch on right

Cross-section A-A of the metal relief illustrated above.

Collage

Interesting group work with children can be based on the use of thin metal foil. Ask the children to collect as many unwanted confectionery wrappings as they can find: sweet papers, Christmas wrappings, cake bands, etc. Assemble a wide assortment with as many brilliant reds, blues, greens and other metallic hues as possible. Sort into colour groups: reds, pinks, crimsons, oranges into one group; yellows and golds into another and so on. Collect together oddments of silver kitchen foil (both shiny and dull sides can be used). Add any pieces of coloured cellophane (also from sweets and other wrappings), of bright 'dayglo' papers and the occasional piece of glossy white paper..

Prepare a large base from the side of a corrugated cardboard bicycle container or from pieces of stiff paper glued together to make a large enough sheet. Paint a dark background (of black or deep blue, for example). Choose a suitably wide topic or theme that involves the idea of brilliance, brightness and reflection: water patterns, fishes, armour, space travel, etc. Stick on the foils and other materials with epoxy resin adhesive (for kitchen foil) and PVA adhesives (for thin wrappings).

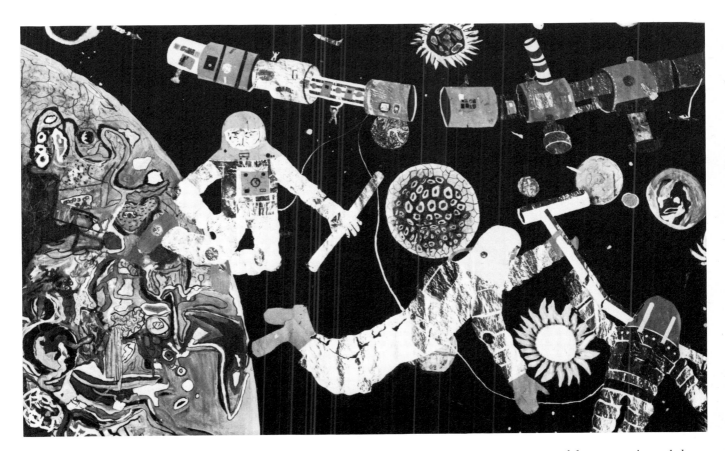

Conquest of Space: a group work 10 ft × 6 ft (3 m × 2 m) involving ten children. The spacemen, suns, parts of the space station and planets were made from foils. Other parts came from coloured papers with some painting (powder/poster paint).

METAL GAUZE

Interesting variations on sheet metals are gauze and other forms of perforated metal. The kinds most commonly found as metal scrap are zinc (a dull grey colour in a disused state) and aluminium (silver bright and more malleable than zinc). Both sheets are relatively thin and can be cut with scissors or jeweller's snips. Perforated steel sheet (silver grey or, in its waste state, often rusty red) is much harder and has to be cut with heavy duty shears, even when it is very thin. These and other kinds will probably be found at local scrap merchants and from some sheet metal works.

The introduction into craftwork of a material with a network of holes offers possibilities for the exploration of spatial relationships, which is particularly useful in design courses when ideas are being worked out for space-shape structures with light, open forms. Sheet steel with very large punched holes may suggest 'windows' through which to view space within and through a structure. The smaller holed gauzes have a semi-transparent quality that offers an interesting contrast to areas of plain sheet metal.

Alternatively, the network of holes may serve to carry rod patterns between 'walls', making a linear plane movement across and through the structure. A useful rod size for standard gauze is the bicycle spoke. (See also page 102 for other uses of bicycle spokes.)

Gauze structures

Experiment with an old sheet of zinc gauze. First flatten out any creases gently and then clean with wire wool, soap and water. (Protect your working surface.) This will restore the original surface and colour of the material. Try out your design ideas with cardboard first (especially if you have only a small amount of the metal) before transferring to the zinc which can be cut out with scissors.

Structures of this kind need not be fixed unless you wish to keep them permanent. The component pieces can be used again to make new shapes and forms. Many three-dimensional theatre structures can be developed from forms like these. Epoxy resins can be used to fix to base.

Left, gauze structure mounted on sheet metal.

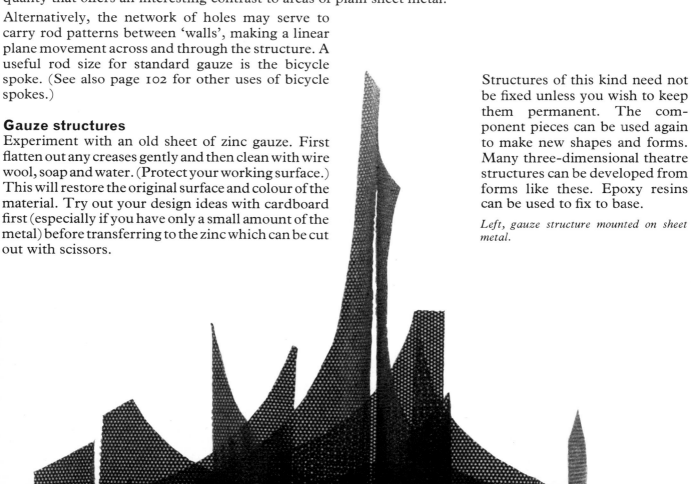

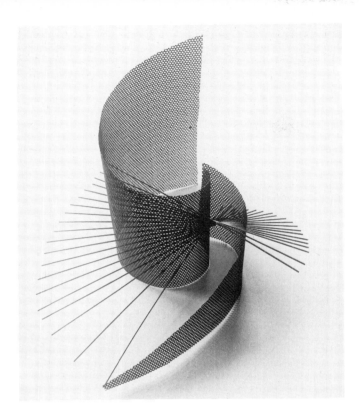

The illustrations on this page show a variety of structures based on sheets with perforations of assorted size together with rods.

The top design was an exercise in spiral linear form using a single piece of gauze cut on the diagonal and folded back. Bicycle spokes (with the ends cut off) were passed through the holes at regular intervals.

The illustration lower left shows another exploration using two of the gauzes in a wheel form with radiating spokes.

The structure below used three rod sizes and three kinds of perforated sheet to form a cylindrical tower.

You can explore many space-shape ideas using this type of material.

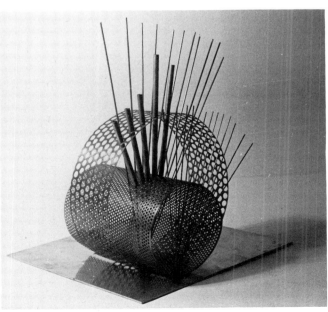

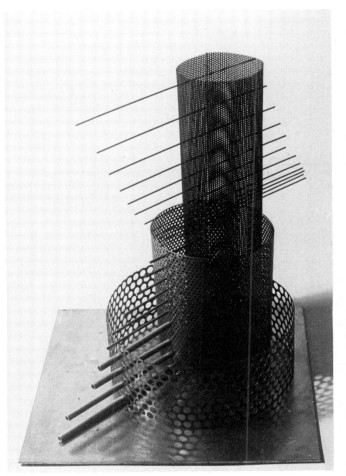

METAL STAMPINGS:
Material and techniques

Sheet metals with shapes punched out at regular intervals are called 'stampings' or 'punchings'. These can occasionally be obtained cheaply from a scrap metal merchant or, if there is one locally, from a metal forming manufacturer (look up the Post Office Yellow Pages under Sheet Metal Works).

Some typical stampings available in Light Industrial Areas:

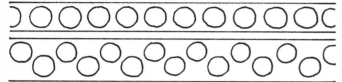

Aluminium foil strip punchings from the manufacture of milk bottle tops. (Bottling plants will be more ready to supply if you return the waste after use – it has some value as scrap, being of pure aluminium.)

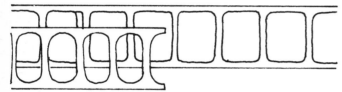

Aluminium sheet in various thicknesses from washers, tags, etc.

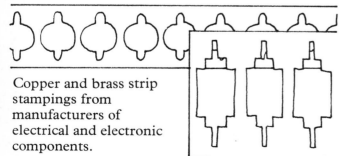

Copper and brass strip stampings from manufacturers of electrical and electronic components.

Steel stampings from sheet metal works – very tough, not suitable for cutting.

Cutting and bending

A length of typical aluminium stamping with about ten large holes can be exploited as a basic building unit if you cut, bend and then join to similar units.

Cutting

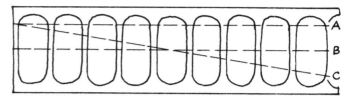

Cutting across the strip at A with a pair of shears will give two patterns:

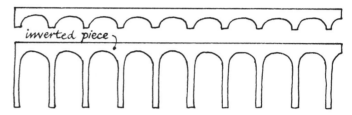

inverted piece

Cutting across at B will make two equal pieces:

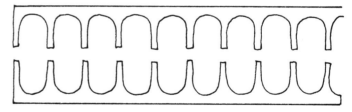

Cutting diagonally across from C will make two equal pieces which can be joined thus (use epoxy resin adhesive for aluminium):

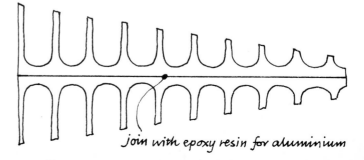

join with epoxy resin for aluminium

Bending

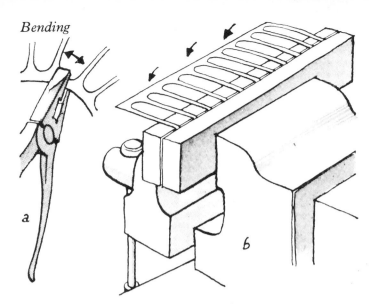

a Strips can be bent at individual points in the jaws of flat-nosed pliers.

b Complete strips can be bent over in the jaws of a vice – clamp between wood blocks and hammer down with another wood block.

Three examples of bending:

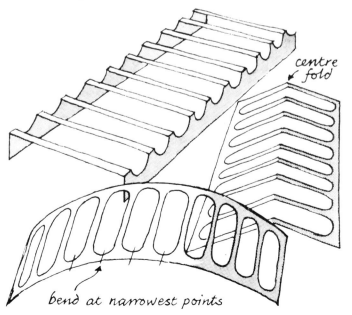

centre fold

bend at narrowest points

Cutting and bending

Combining the two techniques of shaping the unit, cutting and bending, results in a wide assortment of forms:

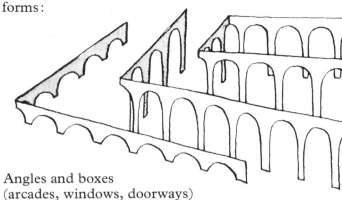

Angles and boxes
(arcades, windows, doorways)

Curves and cylinders
(arenas, circular buildings)

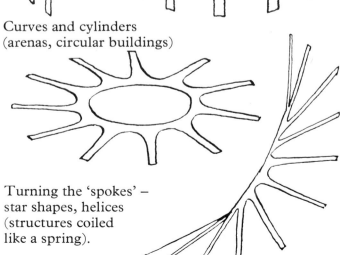

Turning the 'spokes' –
star shapes, helices
(structures coiled
like a spring).

METAL STAMPINGS: Structures

The illustration shows three levels of the kind of stamping shown on the previous page. The strips were cut into lengths of 28 holes, joined at any convenient points with epoxy resin adhesive (Araldite in the U.K.). This stamping pattern has been combined with another at the top to give the narrow holes. (This second pattern is also used along the top of the 'wall' in the foreground.) The bottom edge of the building has been removed so as to give an arcade effect.

Experiments with this type of basic form can be considerable. Try folding to make a variety of polygons:

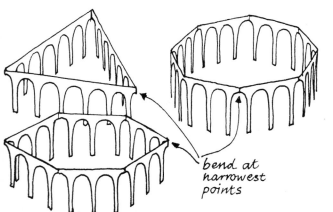

bend at narrowest points

Also try a building of many stories (towers and skyscraper blocks):

Five or more stories in height for church towers and belltowers. Experiment also with the lower stories alongside for naves and aisles.

Circular forms
Using the same kind of stamping, experiment with different curves.

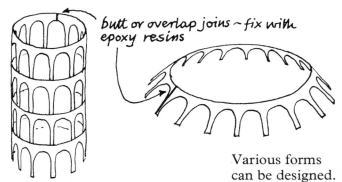

butt or overlap joins ~ fix with epoxy resins

Various forms can be designed.

Type of circular structure with a sloping, domed roof (similar to the Royal Albert Hall, London). For the roofing pieces, cut off the edge from a strip of stamping and gently fold in each 'spoke' whilst bending the outer rim between each 'spoke'.

bend in slightly

bend down slightly

Hanging forms

Another common form of stamping is from thin aluminium foil. This has a limited use as a craft material but can be assembled for hanging Christmas and party decorations because of its shine. 'Gold top' foil provides a useful colour change. Two forms of stamping are available.

Thick wire coat-hangers are ideal for draping and hanging foil. Very large chandeliers can be built over a thick wire hoop (one can be made from two hangers – this has the advantage of providing hooks for suspension).

Hangers in various forms, the one on the right built up from two coat-hangers.

  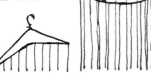

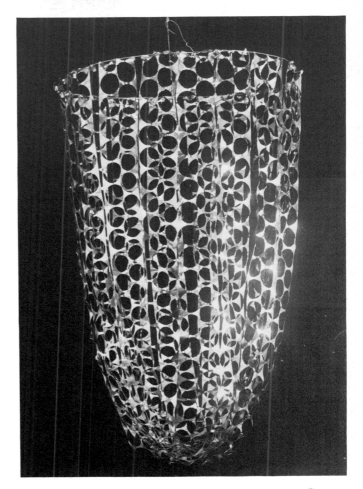

Chandelier built round large wire hoop. Cross-pieces and lamp holders can be fitted inside.

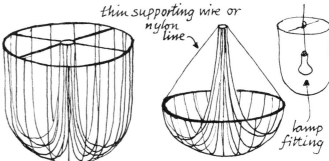

thin supporting wire or nylon line

lamp fitting

Experiment with different forms of chandelier by pulling the centre of the hanging foil upwards.

115

WIRE MESH

Wire mesh (or 'chicken wire') can be found as offcuts or as lengths thrown away because it has been spoilt on farms, building sites, etc. This is a particularly useful material for constructing large, irregular-shaped objects.

The only tools for forming the mesh are snips or wire cutters and a pair of pliers. Gloves are recommended for tender fingers.

Covered with papier mâché, mesh is ideal for making theatre props, carnival masks or bases for geographical or architectural models.

The paper covering method is described on page 58.

Carnival mask

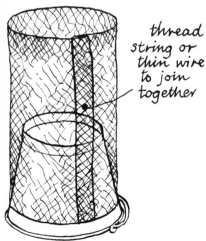

thread string or thin wire to join together

1 Roll a piece of mesh into a cylinder and support on an inverted bucket for stability. Join the mesh by twisting loose ends over each other. Strengthen the join by threading with wire or string.

wire cutters

2 Cut seven or eight vertical slits down from the top edge.

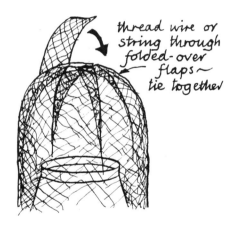

thread wire or string through folded-over flaps — tie together

3 Fold over each flap and secure with wire or string.

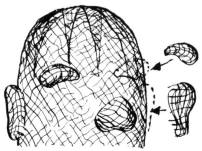

4 Build up features with additional pieces of mesh.

five or six layers of Papier Mâché

5 Remove from bucket and squeeze and pull bottom edge to fit the head and shoulders of the performer. Build up papier mâché. (For method see page 58.)

6 When the head is dry, paint it to suit the character of the mask. Add hair with old rug wool or thick cord. Insert plastic foam or padding to protect the wearer's neck and face. Add four tapes to the wire round the neck as a harness to fit round the waist or under the arms.

string, rug wool etc for hair

eye holes

plastic foam

tapes

7 Cut eye holes to suit the eye height of the wearer. Cover with transparent gauze and paint with thin colour to match other face colours.

Landscape models

Mesh built over a wooden structure and covered with paper or plaster lends itself well to the construction of irregular objects such as geographical landscape models based on relief maps.

If a scale model of a particular area is required, it should be constructed on a base of suitable size made from blockboard or plywood in the case of a large-scale model or from hardboard in the case of smaller models.

There are many scaling methods available. One is to take readings of the different heights and to fix short wooden blocks (to a scale of millimetres to the metre) in appropriate positions on a scale layout drawn on the base board. Secure the blocks by gluing and screwing down.

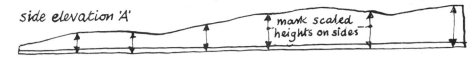

side elevation 'A'

mark scaled heights on sides

Cut out, glue and tack hardboard or card sections to all sides of the base board. These will represent the profiles of height readings from your map. They will serve as a correct level and a fixing point for the wire mesh.

Shape the wire mesh to the tops of the wooden blocks and fix it there. Bend over the top edges of the profiles and secure with small staples or panel pins at base level. Finally apply scrim (hessian mesh) dipped in plaster.

Paper pulp or papier mâché can be applied to fill out hollows and to correct errors in height according to the scale requirements.

Finish off the papier mâché over the entire model. Allow this to dry, sand the surface and then paint and varnish (with matt finish). Details (trees, water, etc.) can be added later.

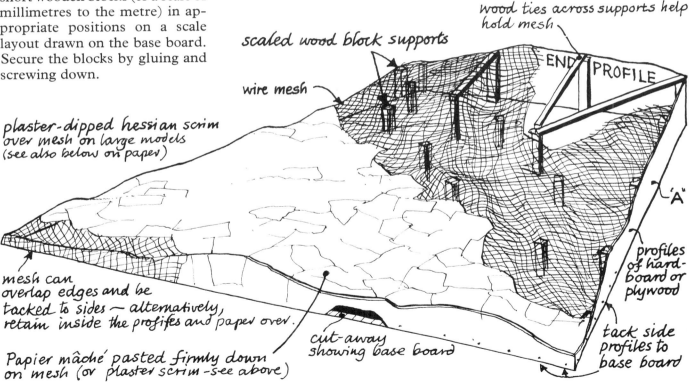

wood ties across supports help hold mesh

scaled wood block supports

wire mesh

END PROFILE

plaster-dipped hessian scrim over mesh on large models (see also below on paper)

'A'

profiles of hardboard or plywood

mesh can overlap edges and be tacked to sides — alternatively, retain inside the profiles and paper over.

cut-away showing base board

tack side profiles to base board

Papier mâché pasted firmly down on mesh (or plaster scrim – see above)

Note: The addition of scrim and papier mâché to wire mesh will add a few millimetres to the height of your model. This should be allowed for when marking off scale on supports and side profiles.

NAILS

Nails are not usually associated with the idea of scrap metal as they can so easily be used for normal practical repair work and stored away for the odd job in the home. However, many large ironmongers and wholesalers in metal components have 'sweepings' at regular intervals in their shops and storerooms. Bags of assorted nails can then be purchased very cheaply.

Very simple nail sculptures can be assembled as shown on the right with a minimum of materials and equipment. For young children epoxy resin adhesive (Araldite in the U.K.) is safe and simple to use for the fixing or joining of nails. Soldering is an alternative for the more advanced.

Soldering

Use a soldering iron (100–150 watts) for small work and a soldering torch for larger work. For use with nails, a soft solder should be applied with a resin flux. Heat and apply solder over a piece of asbestos or some bricks. Always ensure that nails are clean and free of grease before attempting to solder them.

Flat arrangements

For flat arrangements, lay the nails in the pattern required. Apply flux to the joint and apply solder direct to the work with a soldering iron.

The method can be summarised as follows:

1 Clean all parts that are to be heated.

2 Heat parts and daub with flux.

3 Heat the soldering iron. Make sure that the tip is clean by dipping it occasionally in soldering fluid.

4 Apply the solder by melting it on the tip of the iron until it flows onto the joint.

5 For quicker and more effective results with nails use a butane torch – but be careful not to overheat.

6 The residue of solder can be cleaned off in a hot alkaline solution (hot water with soap or detergent) and with a brush.

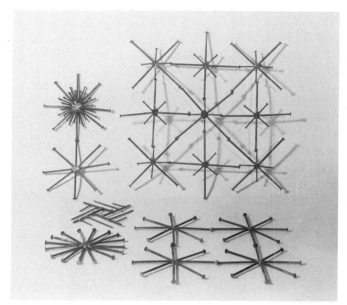

Assorted nail patterns; nails soldered together.

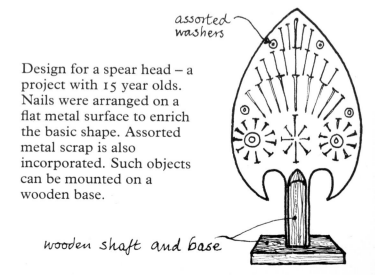

assorted washers

Design for a spear head – a project with 15 year olds. Nails were arranged on a flat metal surface to enrich the basic shape. Assorted metal scrap is also incorporated. Such objects can be mounted on a wooden base.

wooden shaft and base

iron (or torch)

soft solder

heat proof base

Reliefs

If a large quantity of assorted nails is available, it is interesting to attempt a nail relief. The purchase of a few special nails could be considered to complete a particular design project. Nail reliefs are basically two-dimensional designs that rely more on the head shape of the nail than on its length. The nails are hammered into a base of soft wood or, if preferred, of cork or similar soft material glued to a base. Projects of this kind are based on dot patterns. Dot patterns abound in nature (stars, cell structures, wild flowers in a field, etc.) or may be man made. Cell structures are a useful starting point for this type of design: look at the possibilities of depicting what you see on a micro-slide of a plant stem.

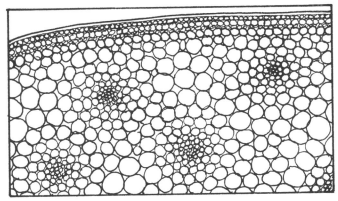

The clusters of smaller cells along the outer surface and inside the stem gradually work towards larger cells. It is advisable to draw simplified sketches of this kind of structure before applying the nails.

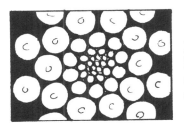

Panel pins in the centre leading to large roofing nails on the edge of the cluster.

Drawing based on micro-slide of a lily stem.

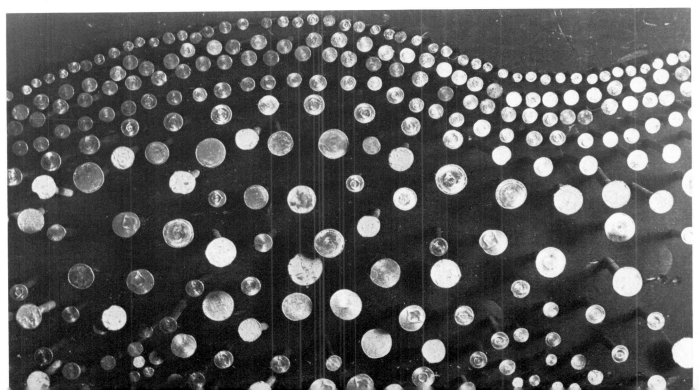

TIN CANS 1

The most plentiful and readily available scrap metal is the vast array of tin cans discarded from most kitchens. There is a wide range of sizes from the shallow salmon tin to five litre oil can.

Colours vary: exteriors are usually dull or bright silver and sometimes printed in solid colours; interiors may be lacquered yellow or bronze. All colours can be used for decorative purposes.

The only essential tools for tin-can work are snips and shears for cutting, needle and flat-nosed pliers for bending and curling, and gloves (old leather or tough cotton) to protect the hands.

Circular decorations

A basic metal forming technique can produce rosettes, sunbursts and other shapes that are suitable for Christmas decorations, stage effects, etc.

1 Remove the top rim of a used tin can, after cutting straight down the side near the soldered joint.

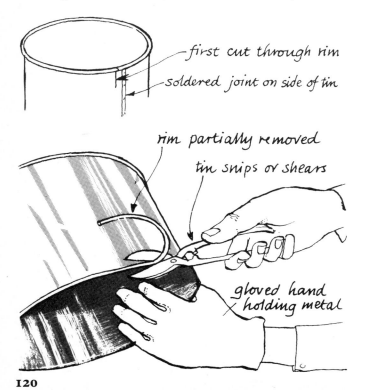

first cut through rim

soldered joint on side of tin

rim partially removed

tin snips or shears

gloved hand holding metal

2 Prepare a paper template by cutting a strip of paper to fit exactly round the tin with a small space above and below. Remove from the tin, fold in half, in half again and then twice more to make sixteen equal sections. Fold again to make 32 sections if preferred. Cut notches at each end of the strip and at each crease line, open out the strip and tape round the tin, ensuring that two of the notches line up with the vertical cut made in 1.

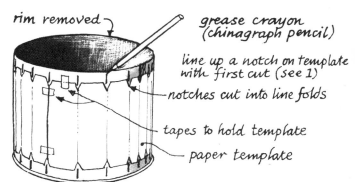

rim removed

grease crayon (chinagraph pencil)

line up a notch on template with first cut (see 1)

notches cut into line folds

tapes to hold template

paper template

Mark with a grease crayon in each notch, remove the template and join all the marks with vertical lines.

3 Cut along the marked lines with light or medium shears – practice on a spare tin will help you to achieve straight or steady cuts. The depth of cut should be to about 20 mm from the bottom rim.

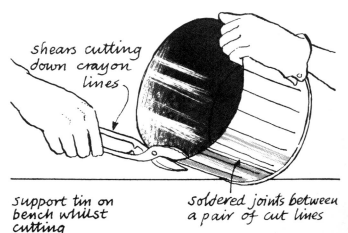

shears cutting down crayon lines

support tin on bench whilst cutting

soldered joints between a pair of cut lines

4 Pull out a strip of tin at right angles to the side of the can with pliers or gloved hand. The strip can be slightly curved, or curled at the end with a pair of needle-nosed pliers. Bend each strip to match the first one.

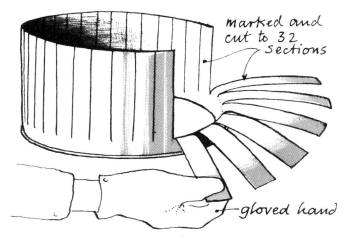

When all the strips have been pulled out, the basic star shape is complete.

5 Try variations on the basic vertical cuts:

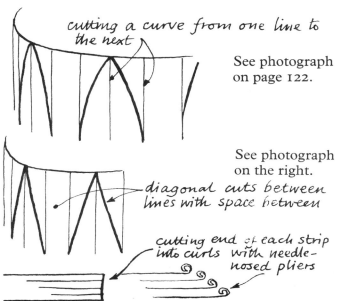

See photograph on page 122.

See photograph on the right.

Collars

If the base of a used tin is removed from inside its rim, an open cylinder is formed. This will form a circular decoration like a collar. Mark and cut as described for the basic star shape but cut right down to the base rim.

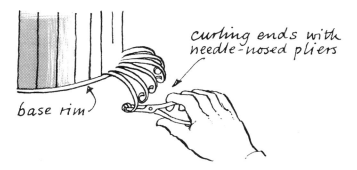

This collar can be used as an additional central part to a bigger circular design.

A large preserve tin made into the form of a collar with diagonal cuts and the strips folded back at two levels.

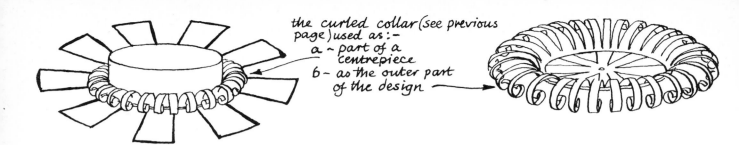

the curled collar (see previous page) used as :-
a ~ part of a centrepiece
b ~ as the outer part of the design

A selection of stars, sunbursts and geometrical circular forms based on tin cans. Note the variety of shapes and the use of alternating spokes. The central design has been worked over with a metal punch.

Plastics

5

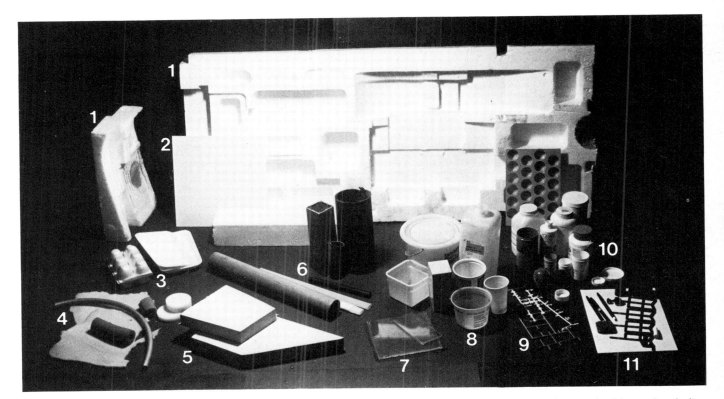

1 expanded polystyrene packing cases and containers; 2 ceiling tiles; 3 food containers; 4 plastic foam sheet and tubing; 5 insulation panel offcuts; 6 PVC tubing and drainpipes; 7 acrylic sheet; 8 assorted food and drink pots; 9 plastic model kit offcuts; 10 pharmaceutical containers; 11 assorted plastic oddments (felt-pen holders, etc.)

PLASTICS

Under the general term 'plastics' can be found a very wide range of man-made waste material. It is used chiefly in the retail trade as a packaging and display material and for insulating and plumbing in the building trade.

Different types of plastics can produce such a vast variety of forms and structures that I have for convenience grouped the plastics into four main types:

1 expanded polystyrene, which is white, light-weight and rigid
2 polystyrene or polyethylene, from thin containers (food, drink and drug)
3 polyurethane foam, which is soft and flexible
4 acrylic sheet ('perspex'), which is rigid, hard and clear – similar in appearance to glass.

Sources of supply

Expanded polystyrene is preformed. Motorcycle showrooms are likely to have motorcycle packing cases which will give large forms with interesting internal shapes. Wholesale and retail trade counters in the electronics trade may be able to supply medium sized plastic packing from different types of equipment. Strip expanded polystyrene and small block forms can often be discovered at refrigerator showrooms – the strips are used to protect the edges of large freezers. The home itself should produce a variety of small food containers. Sheet forms of expanded polystyrene can often be found at large department stores as well as other types of container. Enquire of a department manager and arrange a collection time.

Flexible polyurethane foam is not so plentiful but can sometimes be obtained from building sites (offcuts of lagging, etc.), old car seats (particularly suitable for stuffing soft toys) and open markets. Also from certain factories.

Acrylic sheet ('perspex' in U.K.) is occasionally available as offcuts from the glass departments at builders' merchants. The small pieces are adequate for the craft projects shown in this section.

Working area

Only a relatively small space is required for most craft projects illustrated here. However, if you are handling large pieces of expanded polystyrene ensure that you have plenty of floor and bench space and an adequate bin for collecting your own waste – sawing and cutting this material will deposit a mass of fine particles.

If you propose to use one of the heated wire tools, make sure that there is good ventilation as toxic fumes can accumulate if windows are shut. When smoothing the surface with sandpaper, wear a face mask to avoid inhaling fine dust particles.

Try to keep an area for the storage of finished work. A long shelf against a wall is suitable. The shelf and brackets can be very simple and lightweight as there is no weight problem with most plastics.

Tools

(Adhesives are recommended in the appropriate place for each project.)

For expanded polystyrene:
– a sharp modelling or craft knife
– a long metal straight-edge for cutting
– an old hacksaw blade, suitably sharpened on the smooth edge for cutting and sawing (see facing page).
– heated-wire cutters – two types (see facing page)
– stiff card for use as a cutting board

For polystyrene pots only:
– old treadle fretsaw (or small bandsaw if available) for slicing pots.
– hand stapler

For acrylic sheet:
– for cutting, fine-toothed disc on circular saw bench (or similar fixture)
– for shaping, abrasive disc on circular saw

Home-made tools

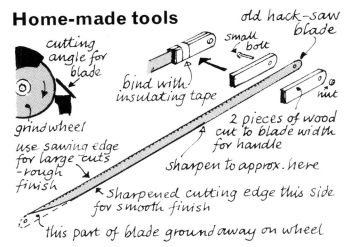

cutting angle for blade

grindwheel

use sawing edge for large cuts -rough finish

Sharpened cutting edge this side for smooth finish

this part of blade ground away on wheel

old hack-saw blade

small bolt

bind with insulating tape

2 pieces of wood cut to blade width for handle

nut

sharpen to approx. here

A Cutting Knife/Saw

Use an old hacksaw blade. Hold it at an acute angle to a power-grinding wheel to get a deep edge for easy cutting. The long narrow point is for detail cutting.

Note: sharpen only up to two-thirds of the smooth edge so that the user may rest his finger on the handle end of the blade whilst sawing.

Heated-wire Hand Cutter

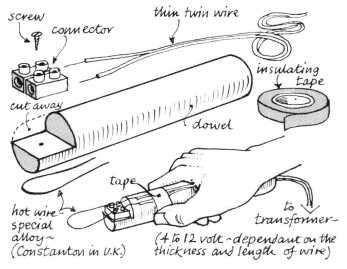

screw

connector

thin twin wire

cut away

insulating tape

dowel

hot wire special alloy~ (Constanton in U.K.)

tape

to transformer~

(4 to 12 volt~dependant on the thickness and length of wire)

Use a piece of 22 mm dowelling for the basic tool. Cut away half the thickness at one end to accommodate a wire connector.

Heated-wire Bench Cutter

For cutting through large, thick expanded polystyrene, and for controlled cutting of straight lines, it is worth building a simple heated-wire cutter that can be attached easily to a bench or table top. The illustration below shows a wall bracket supporting a wood strip to hold the top end of the heated wire. (A shelf over a wall bench could act as the support instead of a wall bracket.)

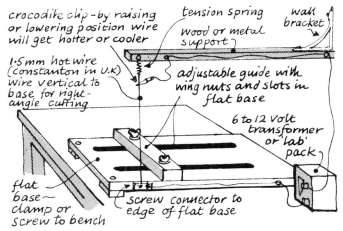

crocodile clip - by raising or lowering position wire will get hotter or cooler

tension spring

wall bracket

wood or metal support

1.5 mm hot wire (constanton in U.K.) wire vertical to base for right-angle cutting

adjustable guide with wing nuts and slots in flat base

6 to 12 volt transformer or 'lab' pack

flat base~ clamp or screw to bench

screw connector to edge of flat base

To cut circular pieces of expanded polystyrene, place blocks of it on a large nail fixed in a plank of soft wood. Turn the block towards the heated wire with a steady movement to produce a smoothly curved surface.

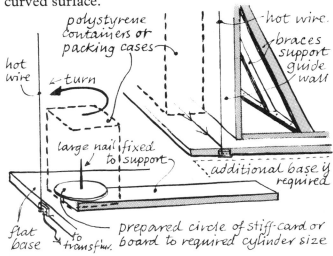

polystyrene containers or packing cases

hot wire

turn

hot wire

braces support guide wall

large nail fixed to support

additional base if required

flat base

to transfor.

prepared circle of stiff card or board to required cylinder size

EXPANDED POLYSTYRENE BLOCK: Cutting techniques

The noticeable feature of expanded polystyrene is its extreme lightness and whiteness. It is made up of close cellular grains of coarse or fine size according to the type of surface finish. The coarse open grain type shown here is ideal for easy sawing and cutting and lends itself to all kinds of sculpture.

Ideas for sculpture can be developed through drawings or rough models in Plasticine or clay – unless you feel confident about working direct on the material.

Two cutting techniques can be tried: with a prepared and sharpened hacksaw blade, or with a heated-wire hand cutter (see previous page).

1 Draw on paper a basic plan (overhead view) of the thing you wish to make. Try to use up all the space. When you are satisfied with your shape, draw it on the block. Two thin blocks can be glued together with contact cement, natural latex or PVA adhesive and can be cut with a knife – but the heated wire must not be used with joined pieces.

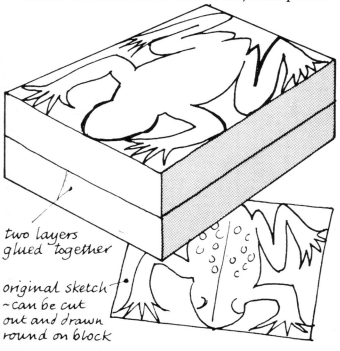

two layers glued together

original sketch – can be cut out and drawn round on block

2 First cut

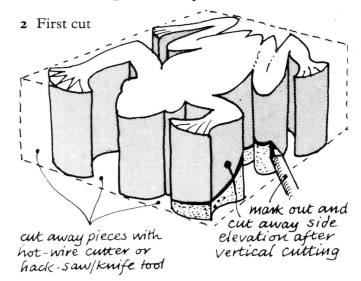

cut away pieces with hot-wire cutter or hack-saw/knife tool

mark out and cut away side elevation after vertical cutting

Two views of frog. Above: basic form cut out with a knife. Below: finished frog before sandpapering and painting.

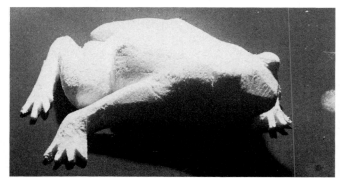

Should you have a long rectangular block of expanded polystyrene, you could attempt the cutting of a large head, perhaps similar to the Easter Island type of monolithic sculpture.

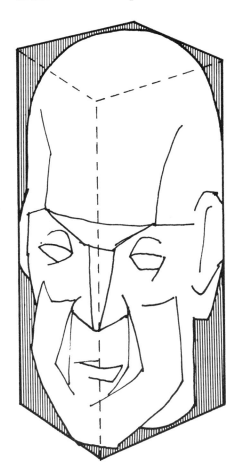

Use one of the long edges for the nose and the centre of the face. Either a heated-wire cutter or a knife can be used here.

The finished carving may be painted with emulsion to simulate stone colour or to create any other colour effect.

Another view of the frog with two other small sculptures. Each piece was made from block oddments obtained from factory sites and trading estates.

EXPANDED POLYSTYRENE BLOCK: Totems and abstract forms

Expanded polystyrene packing cases are pre-formed and complex – ideal for large abstract sculptures. Alternatively they can be cut into medium-sized and small pieces for abstract or naturalistic sculptures, or into yet smaller strips for scale modelling (see page 141). Cutting can be in any direction: straight across (A – A section), straight down through the thickness (B–B) using the heated-wire bench cutter (page 131), or at any other angle. The various shapes that result from such cuts will often stimulate ideas for a piece of sculpture.

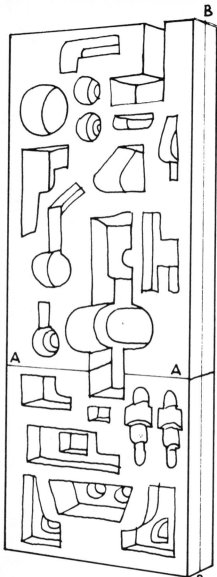

glued joint

added piece

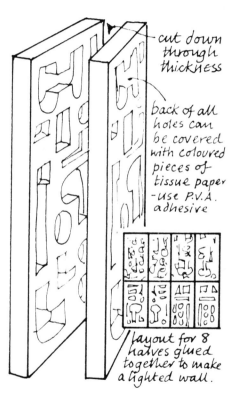

cut down through thickness

back of all holes can be covered with coloured pieces of tissue paper –use P.V.A. adhesive

layout for 8 halves glued together to make a lighted wall.

A typical motorcycle packing case with a variety of hollow shapes to carry parts during transit. In itself not unlike a piece of modern sculpture.

Addition and subtraction: a piece added on the right, other parts cut out. Pieces were glued together with contact cement or PVA adhesive and then to a solid block of wood for stability. Allow at least one day for the adhesive to dry. Such sculpture could be coloured with plastic emulsion or acrylic paint.

The wall of a large packing case sliced through its thickness to produce two pieces of equal length and width. Joined edge to edge, backed with coloured tissue and lit from behind, such pieces can make an attractive pierced wall for screens at parties, discos, etc.

Small abstract sculptures

Large-scale sculptures

Very large pieces can be made from whole expanded polystyrene packing cases. These can be sliced to halve the thickness and to double the number of walls. Pieces can be added or subtracted as required. Group projects can be based on totem poles, robots, would-be computers and assorted space fiction ideas. Glue the pieces together with contact cement or PVA adhesive. Lights can be fixed inside indoor pieces. Work that is to stand outdoors must be weighted to stabilise it. (There are specialist books available for other ideas about the use of expanded polystyrene with concrete.)

As a piece of open air sculpture.

As an interior sculpture, lit from the inside.

A section from an expanded polystyrene packing case can be cut into small pieces for use by a large group. Alternatively pieces discarded from larger sculptures or smaller containers can be used for small sculptures.

The pieces of sculpture illustrated left were suggested by the existing hollows in the plastic. With careful cutting and a final rub with sandpaper simple but effective pieces can be produced – and painted if so desired.

Another use for pieces of expanded polystyrene block is for the making of maquettes if you are trying out ideas before committing yourself to carving in wood or stone.

EXPANDED POLYSTYRENE
Printing 2 – Posters or display work

Large posters and smaller handbills which would benefit from the addition of a design or picture to the lettering can be boldly and effectively printed from expanded polystyrene printing blocks. The lettering itself can be done by hand or typeset if you have a small printing press.

1 Prepare a large printing block as follows:

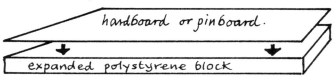

Glue a sheet of thin board to the back of a sheet of expanded polystyrene (approx. 25 mm thick). Use PVA adhesive and allow 24 hours to dry.

2 When the glue is dry, turn over and draw a design on the plastic surface with a felt-tipped pen. Then paint all the areas that are to print the design with fairly thick poster or emulsion paint.

3 Two methods can be used to remove the unnecessary background before printing. As with all printing from blocks, the areas not required for printing must be totally removed or at least reduced in thickness so that they do not come into contact with the ink or paint roller.
a heated-wire cutter combined with a sharp knife for trimming the edges
b burning out with a naked flame (candle) combined with a sharp knife for trimming the edges
For the first method use the heated-wire hand cutter shown on page 131.

4 When the parts not required have been cut and burnt away, the block is ready for the paint roller. Apply a liberal layer of paint (a creamy consistency – emulsion is most suitable) without overloading the roller. Lay a sheet of paper on top of the block and roll over it firmly with a clean roller.

5 Lettering can be direct to the poster paper or on top of the block print when it is dry. N.B. Paper may stretch or shrink slightly because of block printing.

Examples of posters printed from expanded polystyrene blocks. The blocks are on the right.

EXPANDED POLYSTYRENE SHEET : Printing 3 – Wallpaper

Wallpaper designs printed from expanded polystyrene blocks can be very effective. The technique is especially good for large simple motifs. The printing can be done straight onto a wall that has been prepared with lining paper. The wallpaper shown on this page was first painted with plastic emulsion and then rag-rolled in a colour related to the finished print. (To rag-roll, tear narrow strips of old sheeting and wrap round a paint roller with string, tucking ends in and under each other before rolling in paint tray.) The block was printed on top of these two stages of colour.

The block

1 Cutting block

If sharp outlines are required cut with knife before and/or after holding over hot flame

emulsion or thick water-based paint

glue to base with PVA adhesive

EMULSION PAINT

scrap piece of hard/pin board will strengthen soft polystyrene block

2 Recessing unwanted areas by holding the block briefly over a candle.

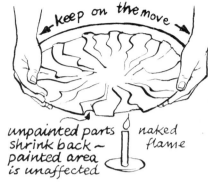

← keep on the move →

unpainted parts shrink back – painted area is unaffected

naked flame

3 Rolling paint across block

roll in both directions to cover printing surface

4 Pressing the block firmly against the prepared wall

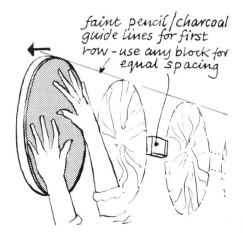

faint pencil/charcoal guide lines for first row – use any block for equal spacing

Architectural and scenic models

Scale models for architectural and drama projects can be satisfactorily made from expanded polystyrene sheet of approx. 20 mm thickness. This is often available from retailers of freezers and other large electrical equipment where it is used to protect the corners in transit. Usually fine-grained in structure, these oddments are ideal for detailed modelling and can be cut with a sharp craft knife – provided some care is taken in the cutting.

The cutting line along the straight-edge should be at a true right angle to the base. The blade of the knife must be kept as close as possible to a horizontal position to prevent tearing. Avoid heavy pressure, especially on the first cut.

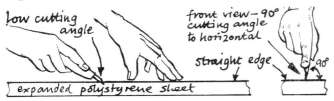

Care with the cutting angle will make for true joins of corners on the final model.

Simple ways of construction:

Steps: a side view showing 4 steps with a top level

Walls: glue edges so that no gaps are visible from front

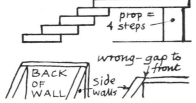

Arches/arcades: either find pre-formed pieces or cut in a curve (see page 131)

Monumental figures, etc.: cut from small blocks using a knife or heated-wire hand cutter – keep as simple as possible.

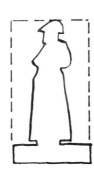

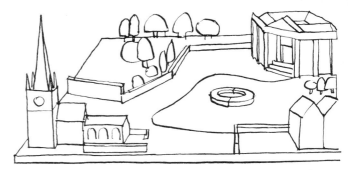

Bases: prepare from plywood or blockboard. Grass and trees can be made from various materials, e.g. grass can be a sprinkling of sawdust on wet glue, trees can be cut from scraps of flexible foam fixed on wire frames (see page 158).

Large group projects can be based on conurbations and industrial complexes. The one essential is a rigid base: use pieces of hardboard (with suitable framing to keep it firm and level) or plywood or blockboard.

Expanded polystyrene sheet can be painted with plastic emulsion or acrylic paints.

Design for a classical drama: scale model setting with arches found among pre-formed packing material, steps cut from sheet, walls made of ceiling tiles.

EXPANDED POLYSTYRENE SHEET: Relief carving

Occasionally larger pieces of sheet may be found. The piece illustrated below came from a building site, a remnant from a new ceiling insulation. Such expanded polystyrene is more dense in quality than the usual open-grain variety and lends itself to heated-wire cutting.

Alternatively, a similar area of sheet could be made up from smaller squares glued edge to edge on a backing of thin board.

Large areas of sheet are ideal for low-relief friezes or similar wall decorations. The starting point could be history or natural history, and the work could be done by a group. If three or more people work on a large frieze, it is worth preparing a set of wire shapes for the heated-wire hand cutter. A wide flat cutter (**A**) can remove all large areas such as the sky, a pointed cutter (**B**) can be used to slip between the folds in the costumes.

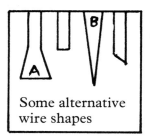

Some alternative wire shapes

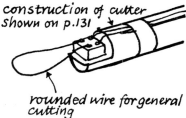

construction of cutter shown on p.131

rounded wire for general cutting

Below, the tool in action. The heated wire is hidden below the surface during a cutting stroke.

Apothecary's sign for a production of 'Romeo and Juliet'

Expanded polystyrene sheet and also, in the U.K. at least, the thin insulating material used to line walls, can make an effective textural covering for scenery in drama productions. Cut in the required shapes and glue them to a set of old stage flats or hardboard backings. Treat all plastic materials used for such a purpose with Albi-clear, a fireproofing solution. This is available through theatrical suppliers.

Other uses

Expanded polystyrene sheet can also be cut right through to make silhouettes and painted to suit a particular design. In the example above the apothecary's sign was cut out of a single 25 mm thick sheet of packing panel and strengthened along the bottom edge with a softwood frame which extends to support the test-tube cut-out on the right.

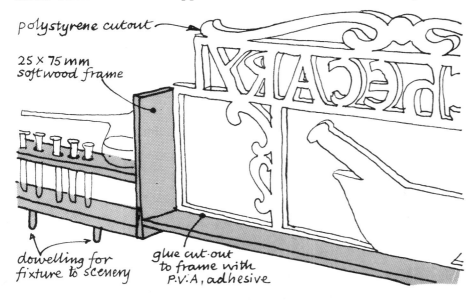

polystyrene cutout

25 × 75 mm softwood frame

dowelling for fixture to scenery

glue cut-out to frame with P.V.A. adhesive

Juliet standing before the wall of the Capulet ballroom in a school production of 'Romeo and Juliet'

EXPANDED POLYSTYRENE CEILING TILES

Complete or broken ceiling tiles can usually be obtained fairly readily from householders or builders who have been using them for a new ceiling or wall. The size and thickness are suitable for individual small cut-out relief silhouettes. For clean edges use a sharp craft/modelling knife; for intricate curving outlines use a heated-wire hand cutter.

This simple cut-out technique lends itself to a wide range of subject matter. Display letters in any style can be drawn and cut out – and used in either positive or negative form.

Experiment with design styles: split up a square or rectangle, balancing that which is removed against that which is left; see the effect of a naturalistic design in this material, or of a Mayan-style classical relief (the edges of the horse and rider illustrated below can be refined or modelled by using a sharp knife after the heated-wire cutter).

Below: designs cut from four ceiling tiles with knife and heated wire.

FOOD CONTAINERS: Trays

Very fine-grain expanded poly-styrene is used for the manufac-ture of food containers (egg car-tons and the type of trays used by supermarkets for meat, fish and tomatoes). The close, smooth and semi-glossy surface texture is easy to cut with a sharp knife and can be glued with PVA adhesive (allow at least 24 hours to dry), or a contact cement or natural latex. Only very small touches of adhesive need be ap-plied.

Support one tray on another for stability and cut into strips lengthwise with a knife and a straight-edge.

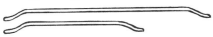

Two basic cross-sections: the length or width of one tray.

Joined together in different ways to form shapes shown in illustration on right.

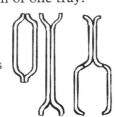

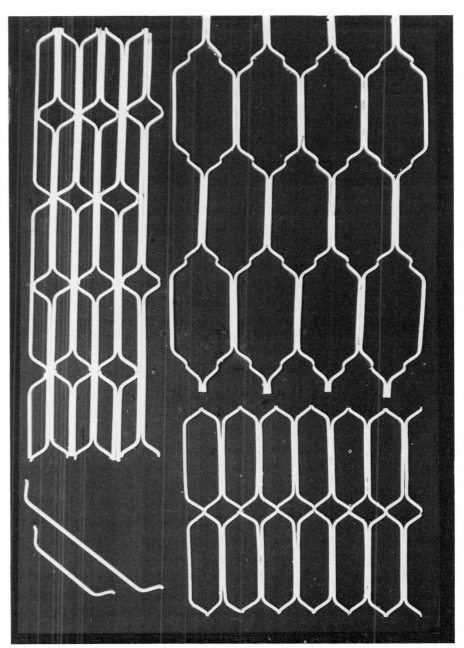

Three patterns using two basic shapes: top left, the longer section dropping halfway on each line; bottom right, the shorter length; top right, the pattern is more complex.

Food containers (continued)
The hanging lantern

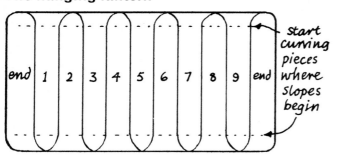

1 Mark out nine or ten pieces across the width of a food tray. The two end pieces will not be used. Cut out the strips, using a spare tray as support.

spare tray as support

2 Glue the pointed ends of strips together to form a six-sided cage with three strips to form the holder.

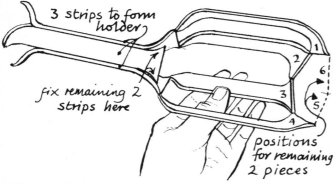

3 strips to form holder

fix remaining 2 strips here

positions for remaining 2 pieces

Chains

Cut widths of different thicknesses (5 – 20 mm) for a variety of forms.

Cut lengthways.

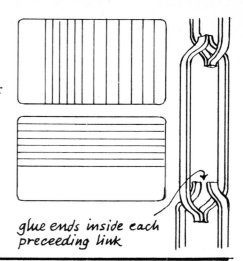

glue ends inside each preceeding link

Ironwork

Reversing the strips alternately and touching the ends with glue will produce shapes reminiscent of Moorish ironwork.

When painted black such a pattern strongly suggests wrought ironwork. The illustration below shows a window built from four corner protectors from freezer packing and two meat trays. It was designed to fit into a stage flat. Alternatively, wood strips could form the outer frame.

back to back and end to end gluing

arrangement of pieces for window illustration on right

Egg cartons

Many of these are made from paper pulp, but some are from expanded polystyrene and can be cut and glued to make party decorations.

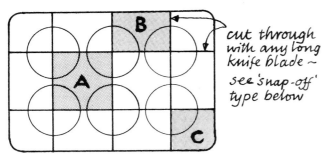

cut through with any long knife blade ~ see 'snap-off' type below

In the plan view, the cutting lines are marked, quartering the dome of each egg shape. The long retractable type of craft knife is most suitable for cutting through such irregular shapes.

'Snap-off' type of knife (also known as 'snap-off' cutters).

cut piece 'A'

cut piece B

cut piece C

Three forms will result from quartering an egg carton: two **A** pieces with four 'petals'; six **B** pieces with 2 petals; and four **C** corners with a single petal.

Experiment with the three forms:

fitting two 'A' pieces together

joining pieces together in different ways

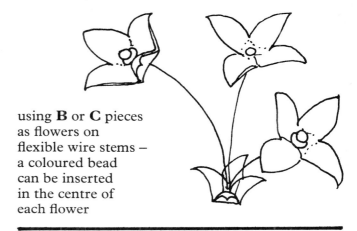

using **B** or **C** pieces as flowers on flexible wire stems – a coloured bead can be inserted in the centre of each flower

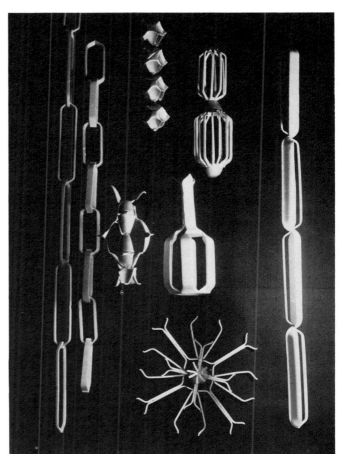

Examples of decorations : on the right, decorations from end pieces combined with cut strips.

147

SMOOTH POLYSTYRENE AND POLYETHYLENE: Oddments

The surrounds from plastic model kits can sometimes be collected in quantity from a group of keen model-makers. These can be assembled and built into a wide variety of linear structures.

Prepare a base of hardboard or thin plywood. Construct on the base a piece of linear sculpture – or perhaps a model of pipe systems based on an industrial oil refinery. All parts can be glued with polystyrene adhesive.

Such frameworks can be incorporated into larger and more complex structures made from a variety of plastic items (see also page 151).

Another form of plastic framing is found in certain kinds of crate, acting as divisions. The example illustrated on the right uses plastic from an old beer crate.

The frame separates the bottles within the crate.

This is made of polyethylene which can be cut easily with a sharp knife. It also has slots which allow parts to be fitted together.

Two linear constructions: above, using waste surrounds from plastic model kits; below, using the inner plastic frame from an old beer crate.

Pots and containers 1

Yoghourt, ice-cream, cleaning fluids and many other liquids are sold in polystyrene or polyethylene containers.

The goblets illustrated right are all made from such containers with various oddments of plastic for stems and bases. If all the parts are polystyrene, use a polystyrene cement for assembly. But if parts are of different plastics, fix with nuts and bolts, wire or dowelling wedged tightly through prepared holes. Lightly sandpaper glossy containers to make a key (rough surface) for painting. Paint with a brown or black undercoat (mixing pigment with an acrylic medium). When dry, paint or spray on a light coat of gold or silver and burnish to give an antique look.

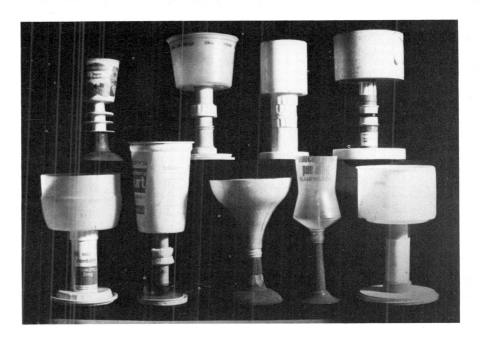

Before and after: nine plastic containers with stems built from plastic cotton reels, litre container caps, containers for adhesive plaster strip and an assortment of lids; the illustration below shows the goblets decorated. Pots and goblets of this type are useful for drama productions and for any kind of display.

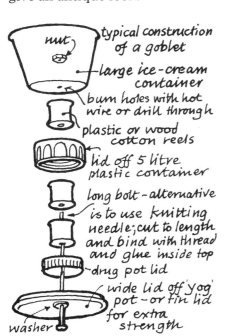

typical construction of a goblet

nut

large ice-cream container

burn holes with hot wire or drill through

plastic or wood cotton reels

lid off 5 litre plastic container

long bolt - alternative is to use knitting needle; cut to length and bind with thread and glue inside top

drug pot lid

wide lid off 'yog' pot - or tin lid for extra strength

washer

SMOOTH POLYSTYRENE AND POLYETHYLENE:
Pots and containers 2

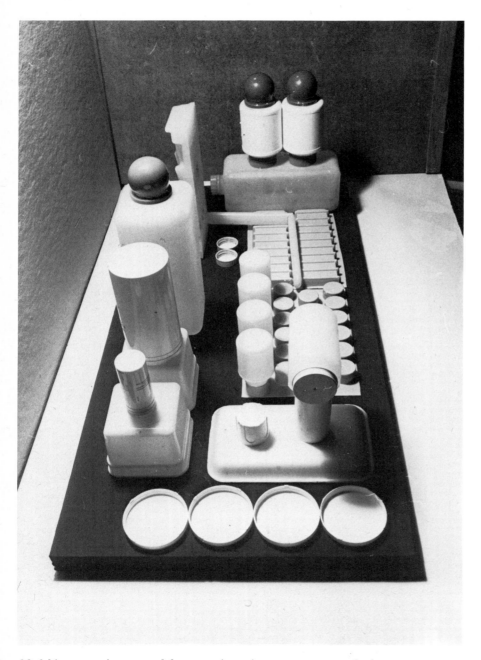

Model incorporating assorted drug containers, ice cream cartons and other pots.

The pharmaceutical trade throws away a vast quantity of plastic pots. Ask at any chemist and make a definite date for collection. Besides pots, bottles and other containers, chemists sometimes throw out old display stands for cosmetics and other products. These are often of preformed plastic.

Pots are of three basic shapes:

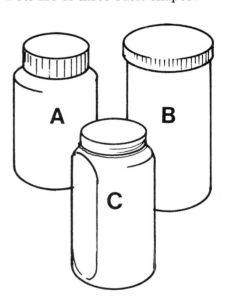

Type A is in two sizes with a screw top and makes an excellent container for glues, paints, etc. in the craft room. Type B comes in five sizes, has a snap-on lid and, in the large and medium sizes, makes an excellent small container for nails, clips, screws and other ironmongery. Type C is flat on two sides and has a metal lid – this is a good shape for joining to other shapes in models.

Oil refineries, industrial sites

Combine plastic pots, lids, bits of display stands, felt-tip pen cases, containers for adhesive plaster strip, and other assorted scrap to build large assemblies based on industrial and scientific complexes (oil refineries, space stations, etc.)

Prepare a plywood or blockboard base to which plastic items can be glued or screwed. Complexity can be heightened by building in 'pipelines' between 'storage tanks' with strips of plastic cut from the surrounds of model kits. Holes can be drilled through pots to take these strips.

Below and right : two examples using assorted plastic scrap. The model below contains cosmetic display stands, drug bottles, polystyrene model kit surrounds, pen holders, square PVC down-pipe, caps from various lotions, finger plaster containers . . .

SMOOTH POLYSTYRENE AND POLYETHYLENE:

Pots and containers 3

Cone-shaped plastic cups and pots can be joined together to make a range of decorations – especially for party use. (Yoghourt pots are often made from polyethylene for which polystyrene cement is no use. In that case, use a hand stapler for joining pots together. Hanging circles, spheres, star clusters and other shapes can all be constructed from this plentiful throwaway product. Try any large institution for a regular supply of cups – caterers may dispose of large quantities every day.

A column

The simplest form to assemble from polystyrene cups is a vertical column.

1 Join cups head to tail with polystyrene cement.
2 Push matchstick with thread through small hole in top inverted cup.
3 If a number of columns are assembled, paint in a range of colours to suit the occasion or setting – use acrylic paints.

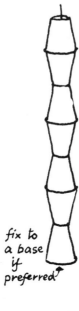

fix to a base if preferred

Rings

You will need 27 or 28 standard size drinking cups (0·2 litre) for a complete circle.

1 Join cups to each other by putting spots of cement at the top and bottom and holding with clothes pegs for 10 minutes until dry.

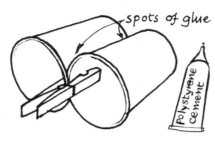

spots of glue

polystyrene cement

2 Alternate the rims under and over in order to achieve a true circle.

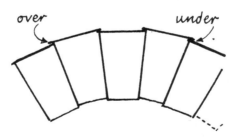

over   under

3 The complete circle.

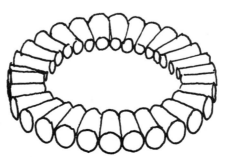

Clusters

1 Take a group of seven even-sized pots or drinking cups. Place one in the centre and arrange the remaining six round it.

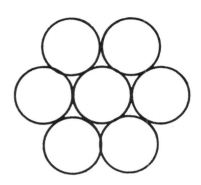

2 Use a larger yoghourt pot in the centre with seven small pots round it – it is possible to retain the rim only for the centre by careful cutting with scissors.

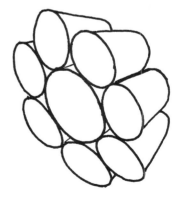

3 The centre can be covered with coloured tissue and varnished to make a strongly coloured centre-piece that will catch the light.

Spheres

Large decorative spheres demand a great quantity of cups. (The two examples that appear on the right were the result of two weeks' throwaway cups from one large school!)

There are two basic joining methods and two types of construction. Polystyrene requires polystyrene cement; polyethylene requires stapling.

Construction 1

The sphere shown top right is assembled by lightly gluing each pot to its neighbours:

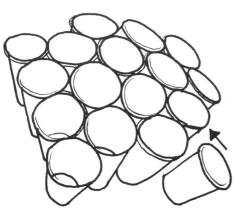

It should be noted that a perfectly shaped sphere is not possible. There will be some gentle pulling or pushing of pots as the sphere gets bigger. Towards completion the spacing will have to get looser. This area can be partially disguised by placing it at the top from which the sphere is suspended.

The peg method of holding until the glue dries is clearly seen in the lower picture.

Constructing spheres, clothes pegs holding pots until glue dries.

SMOOTH POLYSTYRENE AND POLYETHYLENE:
Pots and containers 4

Spheres
Construction 2 : Stapling

Spheres can be strengthened at points by stapling or, in the case of polyethylene pots, stapled entirely. (This is more expensive than one tube of cement for a large sphere.)

Staple the pots together with either a pair of staple-pliers (as shown above) or with a standard hand stapler. In the latter case, support of the base plate will have to be by hand.

Open spheres
Another kind of sphere is one with larger spaces between the cups. This allows more light to shine from the inside and, of course, requires fewer pots. Methods of construction are the same as for closed spheres.

1 First assemble the ring shown on page 152.
2 Assemble rings above and below with alternate pots only.
3 Assemble complete rings above and below.
4 As **2**: the alternate pots should be in line with those in **2**.

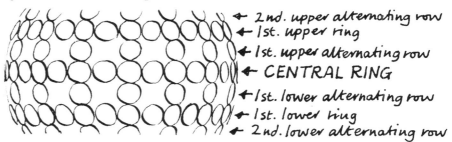

→ 2nd. upper alternating row
→ 1st. upper ring
→ 1st. upper alternating row
→ CENTRAL RING
→ 1st. lower alternating row
→ 1st. lower ring
→ 2nd. lower alternating row

5 Continue as above. There will be occasional misalignments, but with care a complete sphere will result with a little odd spacing at top and bottom. These areas will not be very apparent when the sphere is hung at usual pendant lamp height.

Simple lamp fitting
Use a standard existing ceiling light fitting with bayonet socket. Above the socket fit a piece of tin or a block of expanded polystyrene to support the sphere lampshade. Wiggle socket and support through gaps at top of sphere. One of the larger spaces between the pots is sufficient to insert a small light bulb.

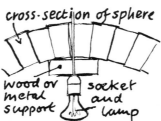

cross-section of sphere

wood or metal support   socket and lamp

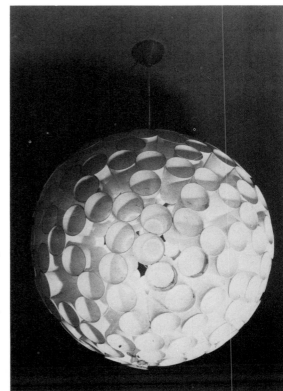

Sliced pots

Polystyrene and polyethylene cylindrical pots can be sliced with the help of an old treadle fretsaw fitted with a thicker blade (a coping saw type is ideal) or, alternatively, by using a standard tenon saw and mitre block although this is a much slower method.

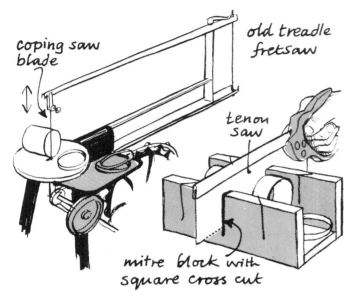

coping saw blade

old treadle fretsaw

tenon saw

mitre block with square cross cut

Mobiles

Cut a wide range of pots into $\frac{1}{2}$ cm or 1 cm slices and arrange in a variety of patterns, hanging by fine threads to flexible wire frames or to wire coat-hangers. Tops and bottoms of pots can be added to the rings. Make sure that the mobile balances as it should. See photograph top right.

Reliefs

Build a suitable base with a simple frame. Paint the base with a strong deep colour to contrast with the white rings. Alternatively, paint the rings with acrylic paints and use light or middle-toned backgrounds. The rings are lightly touched by an impact adhesive at all joining points. See photograph bottom right.

ACRYLIC SHEET
('Perspex')

Narrow strips of acrylic are occasionally thrown away when they have been trimmed from large sheets by retail and wholesale ironmongers, or by builders' merchants. They are usually clear – like white glass – but are sometimes coloured.

Acrylic sheet is thermoplastic, changing from a rigid, tough material to something like rubber when heated. This can be done on the top shelf of a standard domestic oven (electric or solid-fuel) heated to a temperature of between 120° and 170° C (250°–340° F). The time taken will be between 3 and 8 minutes. Temperature and time will vary according to the thickness of the sheet. (The oven door should be closed.)

Shaping heated acrylic

1 Draw a shape on a base of plywood or blockboard. Then hammer a series of oval nails into the base at close intervals of about 50 mm. The nails drawn in black on the picture above are put in later on the other side of the acrylic strip from the first line of nails – to keep the strip in place while it cools. When the first piece is rigid again, as many more strips as required may be fitted round and between the nails.

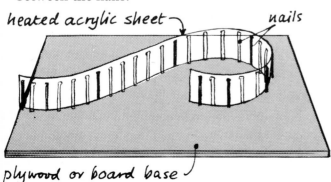

2 Alternatively, in the case of very narrow strips, the material may be heated and then turned and twisted by hand (wear oven gloves!) – and held for a few minutes until the acrylic is rigid.

3 Wider pieces of scrap acrylic can be shaped as follows:

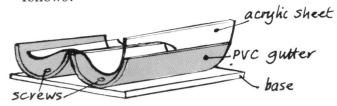

Screw two pieces of PVC guttering (or one piece of drain-pipe cut through lengthwise) to a base as shown. The heated piece of acrylic is laid across the PVC mould and shaped as required by pressing and stretching with oven-gloved hands. This method can be used for narrower pieces, too.

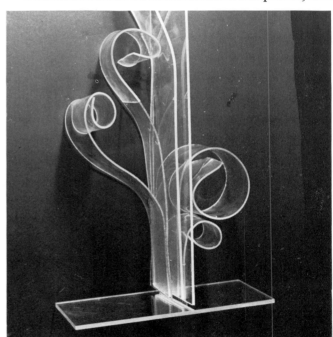

Example of shapes made from acrylic strip.

Machining with saws
Acrylic sheet can be cut with a powered circular saw (with 4–5 teeth per cm) or with a bench-mounted fretsaw (with 5–6 teeth per cm). A home-made protective cover over the circular saw will prevent fine particles from flying about. Hand-held jig-saws may also be used.

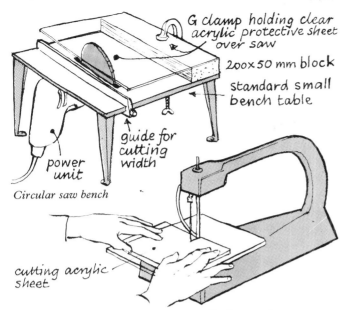

G clamp holding clear acrylic protective sheet over saw

200 × 50 mm block

standard small bench table

guide for cutting width

power unit

Circular saw bench

cutting acrylic sheet

Bench-mounted fretsaw : hold the acrylic sheet as shown.

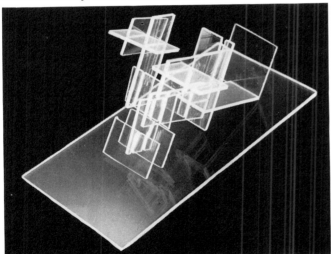

A construction built from small pieces cut from 50mm strips of acrylic scrap with abrasive disc. Each piece has one or two slots cut part way across so that it may fit into other pieces.

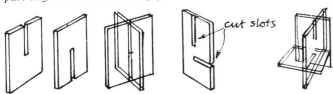

cut slots

Machining with abrasive disc

For curved or straight forms a jig-saw may be used – but better control and finish can be achieved by the use of an abrasive disc attached to a standard power unit.

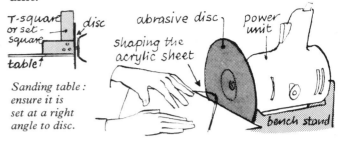

T-square or set-square

disc

table

abrasive disc

shaping the acrylic sheet

power unit

bench stand

Sanding table : ensure it is set at a right angle to disc.

Basic leaf or similar shapes can first be cut with a saw and then finished with the disc. Concave shapes are made by the edge of the disc, convex shapes against the central part of the disc.

Glue with Tensol Cement No. 6 or a similar adhesive.

Try using oddly shaped pieces of scrap acrylic in a variety of forms. For the example illustrated on page 6, some coloured acrylic strips were combined with wood in a linear construction.

Left : plant form using formed strips and cut-out leaf shapes glued to each other and to a base. Right : low-relief panel using similar shapes.

FLEXIBLE FOAM: Animal masks

This is not usually available in large quantities as scrap but may be purchased as remnants or oddments from markets or manufacturers at scrap prices. Occasionally it may be thrown out from packing cases by retailers. Or it may come from discarded cushions or upholstery.

Illustrated on the next three pages are methods of making animal masks from flexible foam, using either adhesive or stitching. Slightly thinned emulsion paint is ideal for decoration.

Lions and tigers

Tiger and lion heads are constructed in much the same manner – the lion will need more 'fur'.

1 Use a squarish piece of scrap foam. Draw the design across the diagonal, as below, with nose, ears and back of head towards the four corners. Alternatively, triangular pieces can be fitted together (by gluing or sewing), and treated in the same way.

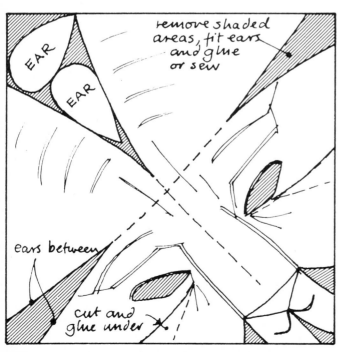

2 The assembled mask will make a form something like this:

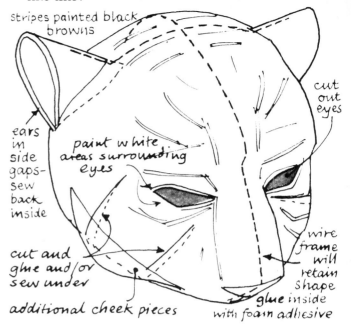

The dotted line represents a wire frame which is there to support and retain the basic shape – this can be glued or sewn in position.

Lion masks will require a number of cut-out surrounds for basic mask.

Eagle mask

The head illustrated below was constructed from two sides, a top, a chin piece, two eyes and some feather oddments. The shapes of these can be varied for other kinds of bird.

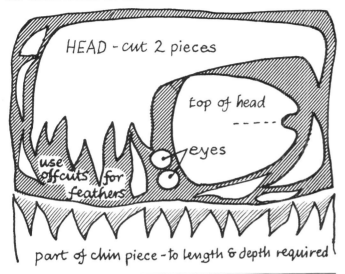

HEAD - cut 2 pieces

top of head

eyes

use offcuts for feathers

part of chin piece - to length & depth required

Completed mask: note the chin piece in place.

Donkey/horse/mule mask

Completed head. The shapes of pieces will vary according to the animal. Broken line shows position of body costume.

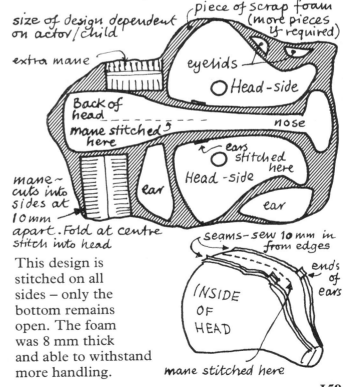

size of design dependent on actor/child

piece of scrap foam (more pieces if required)

extra mane

eyelids

Head-side

Back of head

nose

mane stitched here

ears stitched here

Head-side

ear

ear

mane ~ cuts into sides at 10 mm apart. Fold at centre stitch into head

seams - sew 10 mm in from edges

ends of ears

INSIDE OF HEAD

mane stitched here

This design is stitched on all sides – only the bottom remains open. The foam was 8 mm thick and able to withstand more handling.

Animal masks (continued)

Elephant mask

This large elephant mask was made from six pieces of foam: one for each side of the head and two for each ear. Pieces must be cut to suit the height of the wearer.

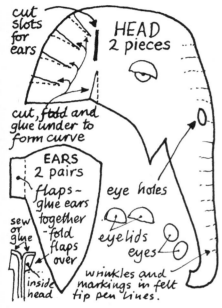

Join the two sides of the trunk with flexible foam adhesive, starting from the tip and sticking first the front edges and then the back edges 50 mm at a time, filling the trunk with scraps of foam to round out the shape.

Sight holes should be cut after marking their position in relation to the wearer. Cover them with coarse gauze or butter muslin and paint the gauze in the same grey as the rest of the head.

All wrinkles and other markings can be drawn in with a black felt-tip pen.

The finished mask. Note the sight holes near centre front. The ear shape and the top of the head are supported by a stiff wire shaped across the head and into the top of each ear.

Miscellaneous scrap 6

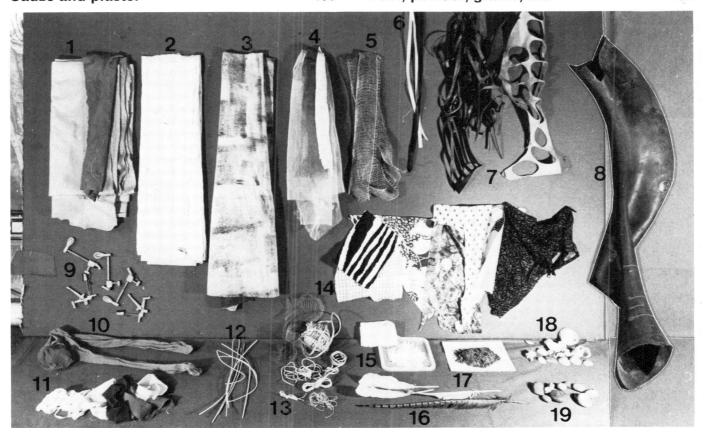

1 felt oddments; 2 sheeting; 3 old blanket; 4 remnants of gauze, net and chiffon; 5 hessian scrim and sacking; 6 old belts, tapes and fabric strips; 7 industrial leather waste; 8 rubber inner tubes; 9 piano parts; 10 nylon tights; 11 assorted fabric remnants; 12 cane; 13 string and cord; 14 assorted printed fabrics; 15 plaster; 16 feathers; 17 sand, sawdust, etc.; 18 shells; 19 pebbles

FABRIC: Batik printing

Pieces of old sheeting (cotton or linen) can be turned into attractive wall hangings, cushion covers and panels for dressmaking if printed by the ancient craft of batik. Pieces of synthetic fabric can be used but sheeting takes the dye particularly well.

Batik is a form of resist printing which uses hot wax. This is applied with a brush for bold simple designs (or with a special pointed tool, a tjanting, for fine lines). The brush is dipped into melted wax and worked over the fabric. The fabric is then dyed and only the unwaxed areas take the colour. Later, the wax is melted out of the fabric which is washed and ironed.

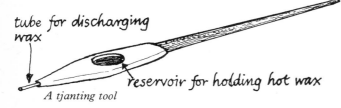

tube for discharging wax

reservoir for holding hot wax

A tjanting tool

1 *Preparing the design*

Choose a piece of sheeting. Make a drawing on a sheet of paper with simple, bold lines. Stylised pictures of animals or plants are suitable, or something geometrical. Beginners are advised to use one colour only: they have only to decide which areas are to stay white (these have to be waxed) and which are to be coloured (dyed).

charcoal

sketch

sheeting or other scrap fabric

Iron the piece of sheeting lightly. Work from your sketch, drawing on the fabric with charcoal.

2 *Stretching fabric*

a After transferring the drawing to the fabric, stretch and pin it to a wooden frame of suitable size and shape. Rest on a worktop well covered with newspaper.

b Another method of stretching (for large hangings) is to use the top of a rough table (a trestle table, for example). Pin the fabric at both ends and then insert strips of wood under the fabric all round the top edge.

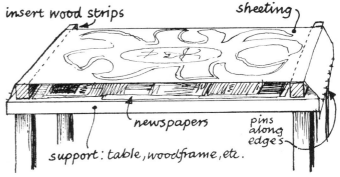

insert wood strips

sheeting

newspapers

pins along edges

support: table, woodframe, etc.

Pinning the fabric

3 *Wax application*

Cut paraffin wax or candle ends into small pieces (or buy prepared wax from a craft shop) and put them into a small tin within a saucepan of water. A quantity of beeswax (1:5) will make the wax less brittle to work. Boil the water over a heater until the wax is melted. Keep the water hot so that the wax remains liquid.

Brush the wax well into your design and leave to harden before removing the fabric from frame.

Some of the equipment and materials

candles

beeswax

paraffin wax

brush

tjanting

4 *Dyeing*

Use an enamel or plastic vessel for a dyebath. Follow makers' instructions for any commercial cold-water dye. Many brilliant colours are available. The more concentrated the dye, the deeper the colour. Try a test piece, allow to dry and judge whether to add more dye or more water.

Dip the fabric into the dyebath for 20–30 minutes, take it out and allow to dry.

Note: the most attractive results will be obtained by using a 'warm' or 'cool' range of colour, i.e. reds / yellows / oranges or blues / greens / purples.

5 Those who decide to repeat the waxing and dyeing processes several times should begin with the lightest colour and end with the deepest, e.g. yellow, then orange, then red, then black. Rinse, dry and remove wax after each dyeing.

6 *Removing the wax*

Place the dyed and dried fabric on newspapers with another sheet of paper on top. Iron with very hot iron, changing the newspaper above and below the fabric each time the iron has passed over the wax. Repeat until all the wax has been absorbed into the newspaper.

Part of a stage setting: old sheeting has been printed in one colour (black) by the batik process.

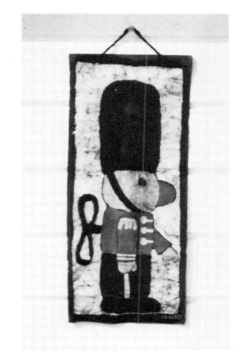

Above and right, two examples of three-colour batik prints. The sun wall hanging has white eyes, yellow face and yellow edges to the rays. Insides of rays and the cheeks are red. The toy guardsman has a white background, black headdress, trousers, turnkey and frame, yellow face, hands and ornaments, and a red nose and jacket.

Details of printing in two or more colours can be found in all books on batik techniques.

MOST FABRICS: Tie-and-dye

All kinds of cloth are suitable for tying and dyeing – remnants of sheeting (cotton, linen or flannelette), towelling, rayon and nylon.

This dyeing technique involves knotting, tying with string or elastic bands and tying round small objects such as buttons or stones which are placed within the material.

Old nylon tights are easy to obtain. The method of tying and dyeing the tights is as follows:

1 Select old tights with as few holes as possible (especially in the leg areas – toes and top matter less).

2 Prepare a mix of 'Dygon' (a commercial product that removes colour from most fabrics) following the maker's instructions. Wash out thoroughly in clean water. Tights should now be in varying tints of pale blue, green and off-white.

3 When dry, the 'bleached' tights should be knotted at regular or irregular intervals up the legs and top. Soak in cold water and lightly squeeze before dyeing.

4 Wear rubber gloves for preparing the dye and stir with a stick. Immerse the knotted tights (and anything else requiring the same colour).

5 Leave for 20–30 minutes for full-strength colour or less for weaker shades. Then rinse in clean water.

6 Untie the knots after dyeing in first colour.

7 Knot again in different positions – and dye in a second colour.

8 Repeat the whole process for each extra colour.

Tie-dyeing inside a nylon stocking
Stuff a length of stocking with any cloth you wish to dye. Tie both ends and pull any surplus over the bundle. Bind with twisted elastic bands. After dyeing remove the bands and the stocking. This treatment will give a variegated finish.

rubber bands

stocking tights

Tie-and-dye decoration
You can make circles by tying areas of fabric tightly round a roughly spherical object before the fabric is dyed. (For the circles on the stage costume opposite, cotton reels were used.)

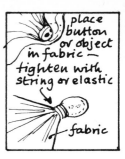

place button or object in fabric – tighten with string or elastic

fabric

The two pairs of tights illustrated above have been made into a stage costume, the top pair being worn over arms and head – a hole having been cut for the head in the gusset.

American Indian costume

This costume is made entirely from an old sheet decorated by the tie-and-dye technique.

1 Start with the basic T-tunic described below. Measure to mid-calf or ankles for women, to mid-thigh for men.

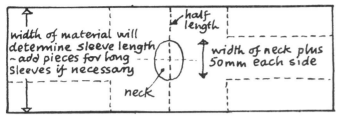

Cut material twice the desired length (or join two pieces). Make a neck hole in centre to width of neck +50 mm each side.

2 Allow 100 mm from hem and 75 mm from bottom of sleeve for fringing. Cut with scissors at 12 mm intervals.

3 Leggings are tubes of the same sheeting –

a Measure under the foot from back of knee to toe (**A**). Then round the leg just below the knee (**B**), adding 12 mm.

b Mark these dimensions on the sheeting, cut out twice and sew the long sides together with a 6 mm seam to form a tube (**C**).

c Sew across one end of each tube (**D**) to form the feet.

d Take two pieces of string or tape at least twice the length of the tube and dyed to match costume. Fold in half and sew the fold to each tube under the toes (**E**).

e Criss-cross the strings over foot and leg up to the knee – then tie off (**F**).

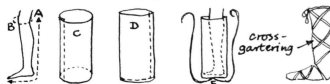

4 Headband: **a** Measure round the head over the brow, adding 50 mm. Cut fabric this length ×75 mm wide.

b Fold to half width. Sew long sides together.

c Place round head, mark and sew the ends for close fit.

d dye the headband if it is to be coloured.

e Sew a feather to the band at the back or front of the head if required. Beads can also be added to the band for decoration.

5 Hair: for a more authentic Indian style than illustrated here, plait long hair or make plaits from old tights or stockings (three legs per plait) and sew them onto headband.

Squaw: the costume is completed by a leather belt and bead necklaces.

MOST FABRICS: Stage costume

Jumble sales are the source of many materials suitable for stage costumes. Discarded clothing can provide brocades, taffetas, lurex fabrics and pieces of fur. Old sheets and curtains (whether solid or sheer) can be used plain or dyed for a variety of clothing. The type and colour of the material determines the status of the wearer though the basic shapes may remain the same.

Medieval man

This costume is made from a variety of fabrics: the tunic from an old lurex dress; the cloak from a piece of large-patterned curtain with a collar trimming of gold lamé from another jumble sale dress; a pair of coloured tights; and the hat – a 'chaperon' – from the same source as the tunic.

Eighteenth century woman

The bodice and skirt are made from an old bridesmaid's dress with paniers of old taffeta, the flounce from a piece of sheeting and the headdress from a rectangle of nylon net gathered and sewn onto an Alice-band.

FABRIC SCRAPS: Collage

Collage is the application of materials to a backing with glue or other adhesive. Almost anything can be used for this technique. Many artists combine it with areas of paint.

All kinds of fabric can be used for collage. Save scrap oddments until you have sufficient of a particular kind for a particular picture. Fix them to a fabric backing with a suitable adhesive (latex).

Backing
Collages are often used as wall-hangings. The backing fabric should fall well and carry the weight of the collage fabrics without sagging. Hessian or burlap is useful. Felt can be used but it should first be lightly glued to card or hardboard.

Right, an Easter Bonnet – the backing is of felt, hat and collar of remnants from dress fabrics. Bits of ribbon could be added.

Below, industrial waterfront – the starting-point for this collage was the vigorous pattern of the broken stripes which suggested water; buildings are of plain and check scraps, the smoke of nylon net.

FABRIC SCRAPS: Appliqué for home furnishing

Appliqué is an embroidery technique where fabric shapes are sewn onto a backing with embroidery stitches adding to the decorative effects. Any materials can be used. For the most attractive results use patches of material on contrasting backgrounds.

The fashion for the 'thematic' approach to decorating allows good use of fabric scraps. The illustration of the kitchen set shows a table cloth which was a good piece from an old sheet and all items with appliqué made from scraps of old sheeting and scraps of polyester fabric from a worn-out pair of trousers.

The theme here is mushrooms and flowers. The cut-out shapes are first machine-stitched on all edges to prevent fraying and then 'appliquéed' to the backing with marline or stab stitch. Most shapes are improved by simple embroidery stitches. The motifs on the cushion are padded with scraps of nylon.

Basic shapes for kitchen set

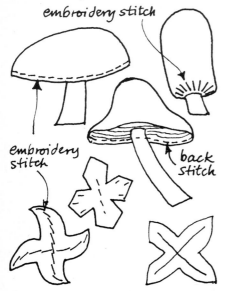

Appliqué on clothing

The use of appliqué may give new life to old clothes – or at least give them a livelier look.

Skirts

Jumble sales often provide ties that are still in good condition. (You will have to cut away the neck section.) One way of using them is as appliqué on an old skirt.

Hemming or overstitching can be used to sew the ties to the skirt, but it must be small and neat.

ties sewn under waist band

contrasting plain colour background

alternating tie arrangement

Blouses

A plain white blouse or shirt can change its character if collar and cuffs are covered with, say, tiny flowers from the border of an old tablecloth, or strips of gingham.

Bolero of plain woven material with felt appliqué flower shapes.

Boleros

The bolero shown in the illustration above can be made from any firmly woven fabric. The appliqué design is a random layout of multicoloured felt flowers in reds, oranges, blues and whites linked by leaves in two tones of green. The flower shapes have been embroidered with thick wool in a weight to complement the bolero fabric.

(The long skirt is of patchwork and is described on page 170.)

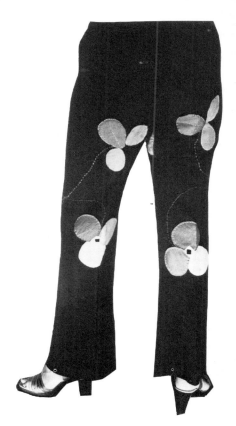

An old pair of trousers made wearable and more decorative by a design of appliqué flowers and embroidery.

Trousers

The trousers illustrated above had holes in the knees and the seat. It was decided to make a contrasting light-coloured design of appliqué flowers and embroidery against the dark blue fabric.

The trousers have flowers 'growing' out of flower pots on the knees and climbing round the legs and seat of the wearer. Simple embroidery in wool and coton à broder links the petals and heightens the colour effect.

FABRIC SCRAPS: Patchwork

Patchwork is made from small pieces of fabric cut to various geometrical shapes and joined to make a patterned cloth.

Originally this technique was developed to make use of sound pieces of fabric from old clothing and furnishings. Large pieces of patchwork were often the result of group activity, notably in the United States of America where 'communal quilts' reached a high peak of artistic excellence.

Making a quilt

The quilt illustrated right was made by a primary school group working in four smaller groups.

1 Group 1 cut a few hexagonal templates from thin card (cereal packet). They drew round the templates on newspaper and then cut out lots of newspaper hexagons.

2 Group 2 used the paper hexagons to cut out fabric.

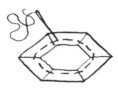

3 Group 3 folded over the fabric and newspaper together by approx. 12 mm on all sides and tacked all round.

4 Group 4 (which had more confidence in sewing) joined all the pieces by oversewing on the wrong (newspaper) side. The tacking was then pulled out and the newspaper removed.

5 The whole patchwork was then mounted on a plain piece of material and lightly hemmed round the edges.

Note: More information about simple and more advanced patchwork techniques can be found in many craft books.

Some patchwork shapes

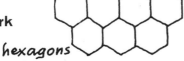
hexagons

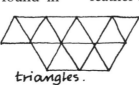
triangles.

Large hexagonal patchwork quilt – group activity by primary school children at Wootton Wawen, Warks.

Skirt (see illustration page 169)

The basic patchwork shape is an equilateral triangle placed in single patches of one fabric or in pairs of the same fabric to make diamonds. The fabric used is furnishing velvet from an out-of-date sample book. Patches have been machine-stitched together and then overstitched along the seams with wool in a feather stitch. Try other patchwork shapes.

diamonds
combined diamonds and hexagons

FELT SCRAPS:
Small toys and mobile

Old felt pieces are very suitable for small soft toys – but other fabrics can be used provided that pieces are machine-stitched together or on edges to prevent fraying. Animal bodies should be tightly stuffed with old tights cut into tiny pieces but all other parts can be from a single layer of felt. Decoration can be embroidery (on the toys illustrated here back stitch, stem stitch, blanket stitch and variations on the chain stitch were used) or the addition of bugle beads and sequins.

In the example shown here two cockerels, two horses and two smaller birds should be made for the mobile. (The cockerel's comb is also stuffed.) The frame is made from a wire coat-hanger and bound with bias-cut fabric.

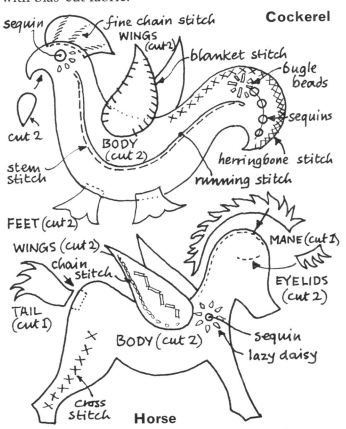

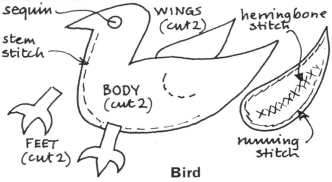

Doll in bed: all the items have been assembled – the eiderdown can be switched with the bedspread if preferred.

FABRIC SCRAPS:
Group toy-making

The doll-in-bed illustrated here
was made largely from a dress

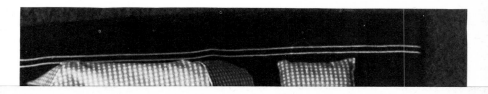

FABRIC SCRAPS: Apple doll

The making of apple dolls is an old American craft. After the harvest an apple would be peeled finely and have a face carved on one side with a blade (a modern craft knife is suitable). Cloves were stuck in for eyes and the apple was left to dry for a week. If the apple is dried in a slow oven the process is speeded up but the resulting face is orange in colour and very much wrinkled – ideal for an 'old granny' doll! (An alternative to this apple head can be made with a piece of felt, folded in two, sewn and stuffed – features are then embroidered on it.)

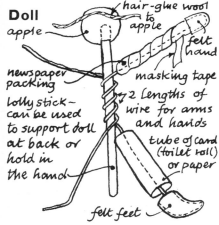

Doll

1 Take a short, smooth stick (an ice lolly stick is ideal) and push it into the apple.

2 Twist some stiff wire round the stick to make a frame for the body. Secure with masking or insulating tape.

3 Pad out with newspaper bound round the wire with more tape.

4 Hair is built up from pieces of wool glued onto the dried apply with Evo-Stik impact adhesive or Bostik No. 1.

5 Hands and feet are made from oddments of felt.

Clothes

In this example black velvet and white lace made the hat; checked linen the blouse; patterned wool and lace the skirt – all sewn to the back of the doll.

Apple doll : the necklace was made from bugle beads – the lace of the hat was gathered and sewn to a scrap of black velvet and fastened on top of the woollen hair.

174

Toy bear

This toy bear has a body and ears of red felt, trousers and braces (optional) of scrap woollen fabric, bow tie of stripes, eyes and nose of felt scraps and a stuffing of old nylon tights.

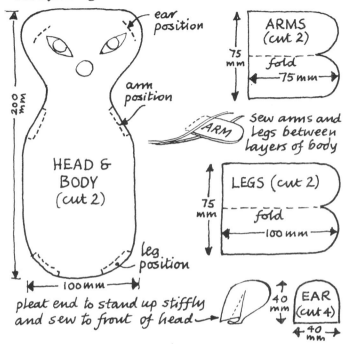

ear position

HEAD & BODY (cut 2)

200 mm

100mm

arm position

leg position

ARMS (cut 2)

75 mm

fold

75 mm

ARM

Sew arms and legs between layers of body

LEGS (cut 2)

75 mm

fold

100 mm

pleat end to stand up stiffly and sew to front of head →

40 mm

EAR (cut 4)

40 mm

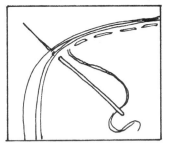

Stab stitch – pull straight through.

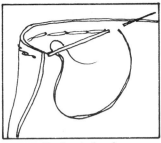

Back stitch – for strong seams.

Toy bear : clothes are optional – other kinds could be designed.

Patterns (not to scale)

1 Cut out pieces. Sew with a stab stitch on the right side or, if the fabric is likely to fray, with back stitch on the wrong side – which will mean turning the toy right side out.

2 Arms and legs: fold and sew along sides and rounded ends. Stuff through open ends and sew up.

3 Sew together body/head pieces, incorporating arms and legs at the positions shown above. Leave unsewn between the two legs.

4 Stuff the body with bits of old nylon or plastic foam – and then sew up the gap.

5 Sew the ears and fasten them towards the front of the head at the positions shown above.

6 Sew on (or glue with Copydex) eyes and nose.

GAUZE AND PLASTER

Occasionally it may be possible to obtain small pieces of plaster bandage that have been discarded. Home decorating often leaves small amounts of builder's plaster and certain modelling kits use Plaster of Paris.

The bird group illustrated here was made from some pieces of plaster bandage dipped in water and moulded over the wire frames. It could also have used strips of muslin or gauze dipped in wet plaster.

Framework

1 Use a square of plywood, chip or block board for the base and stiff wire for the frame. Drill small holes with a hand drill to take the leg wires.

2 Tie in wire of medium and light gauge to form bodies and limbs of the animal you choose to make.

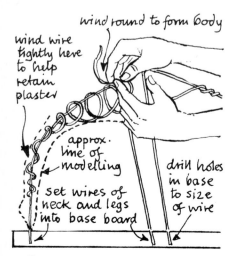

wind round to form body

wind wire tightly here to help retain plaster

approx. line of modelling

set wires of neck and legs into base board

drill holes in base to size of wire

Plaster bandage offcuts

The bandage is impregnated with dry plaster and only requires dipping in clean water. Pull gently over the rim of the bowl to remove surplus water. Then mould to frame. (Both methods leave a rough surface which should be smoothed with a thin coat of plaster before any painting.)

water

plaster bandage

Plaster mixing

Sprinkle dry plaster into small quantity of water and mix to a thin cream. Dip strips of gauze or muslin in the mixture and then mould round frame.

(Plaster is also needed for paper pulp – see page 59.)

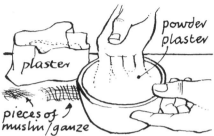

powder plaster

plaster

pieces of muslin/gauze

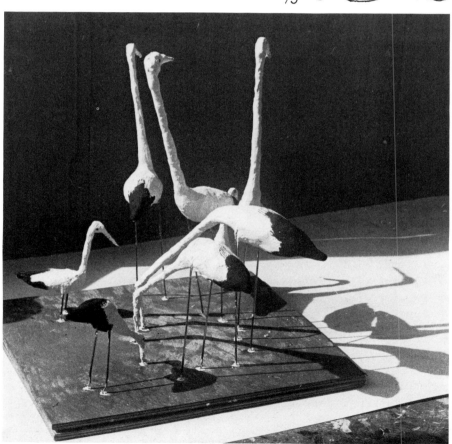

WOOL ODDMENTS: Ojos

Ojos ('God's eyes') are in Mexico a traditional protection against evil in the house and family. The making of them is an ancient craft. Coloured wools are bound round sticks tied in a variety of arrangements for wall hanging. The illustration below shows the most basic form – a cross – to which small sticks have been added at right angles near the tips. Alternative constructions include the Maltese cross which has one vertical and three horizontal sticks, and a mobile where the horizontal sticks are tied in different directions from the vertical, making a three-dimensional form.

Construction

1 Join two sticks at right angles and tie firmly with string.

2 Tie wool to just above the string (**A**) and pull down over stick (**B**).

3 Bind once behind (**B**) and pull over and behind stick (**C**).

4 Repeat binding over and behind stick (**D**).

5 Repeat all round any number of times. Use different colours for a more vivid effect. 'Tie off' wool by tucking in rear and fixing with a spot of Copydex.

Possible arrangements of sticks.

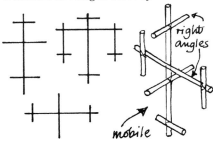

One example of ojos, a simple cross shape using two garden canes with smaller pieces tied on the arms. Three colours of wool have been taken from an old brightly-coloured sweater – the wrinkles add texture.

177

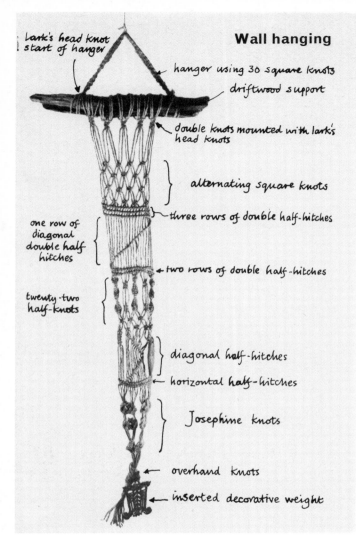

Wall hanging

- lark's head knot start of hanger
- hanger using 30 square knots
- driftwood support
- double knots mounted with lark's head knots
- alternating square knots
- three rows of double half-hitches
- one row of diagonal double half hitches
- two rows of double half-hitches
- twenty-two half-knots
- diagonal half-hitches
- horizontal half-hitches
- Josephine knots
- overhand knots
- inserted decorative weight

The old fisherman's craft of macramé (making nets from string by plaiting and knotting) has been adapted recently for wall decorations, clothing accessories, hanging plant-pot holders and dance masks. According to purpose, any string, cord, rope or heavy wool can be used. Equipment is minimal: a packet of T-pins and a hook on which to hang work in progress.

The following description is sketchy. It is advisable to refer to one of the detailed books on macramé technique.

STRING: Macramé

Materials

The hanging illustrated left was made from 53 yards of 3-ply jute (any string could be used) with a piece of driftwood as the top cross-piece and one or two ornaments.

Hanger construction

1 Cut 2 cords, each $3\frac{1}{2}$ yards long – fold in half.
2 Mount the 4 thicknesses at one end of the wood, with lark's head knots.
3 Tie 30 square knots.
4 Tie ends round other end of wood with an overhand knot and weave them into hanger with a tapestry needle.

Macramé pattern

1 Cut 10 cords of 12 ft 9 in each. Fold each in half.
2 Tie each onto wood with lark's head knot.
3 Count the 20 cords into 5 groups of 4.
4 Tie two square knots with each group.
5 Leave 2 in and then tie 4 rows of alternating square knots with $\frac{1}{2}$ in between rows: *1st row*, divide into groups of 4: 1–4, 5–8, etc. *2nd row*, miss out 1–2 and 19–20 and divide into fours, 3–6, 7–10, etc. *3rd row*, as 1st. *4th row*, as 2nd.
6 Use the left-hand cord as a holding cord and tie 3 rows of horizontal double half-hitches.
7 Use the right-hand cord for the holding cord and tie one row of diagonal double half-hitches.
8 With the holding cord again on the left, tie two rows of horizontal double half-hitches.
9 Again divide the cords into 5 groups of 4 and number them 1 to 5 from left to right.
10 With groups 1, 3 and 5, tie 22 half knots, each with two fillers.
11 With groups 2 and 4, leave $\frac{1}{2}$ in before tying 2 square knots and another 1 in before tying 2 more.
12 Leave $\frac{1}{2}$ in. Tie a row of square knots on 4 groups of 4 cords (cords 3–18 of the 20). Leave another $\frac{1}{2}$ in and tie a further row of square knots on 5 groups of 4 cords (dividing the 20).

13 Tie five square knots on cords 1–4 (of the 20) and also on cords 17–20.

14 With the 12 central cords (5–16) tie diagonal double half-hitches from left to right (using cord 5 as the holding cord) and then from right to left, using the same cord as the holding cord.

15 Taking cord 1 as the holder, tie 2 rows of horizontal double half-hitches across all the cords.

16 Leave 1 in. Divide the 20 cords into 4 groups of 5. Tie each group with a Josephine knot.

17 Leave 1 in. Tie an overhand knot with cords 1–10 and another with cords 11–20.

18 Gather all cords together. Tie 2 overhand knots.

19 Use left-hand cord to wrap all other cords to a depth of ½ in – weave this end into the bundle with a tapestry needle. Clip the remaining cords 2 in below the wrapping.

20 Add ornaments at the bottom and beside the diagonal double half-hitching – or anywhere desired.

Macramé terms

Alternating – a term used when in 1st row all cords are being worked in groups of 4 for square knots or half knots. On 2nd row, the knots are formed from the two right-hand cords of one group and the two left-hand cords of the neighbouring group.

Fillers – the central cords round which other cords are tied, as in square knots, half knots, Josephines.

Holding – a cord that travels horizontally (or diagonally) and onto which other cords are tied, as in double half-hitches.

Wrapping – tying all cords together by winding one cord tightly round all the others.

Gathering – taking a single cord once round the other cords and tied, usually before *wrapping*.

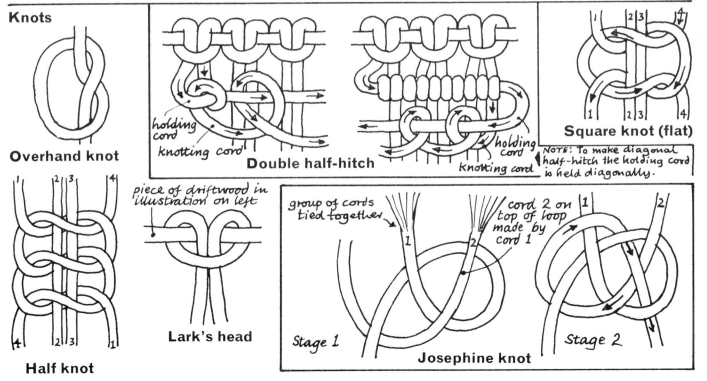

Knots

Overhand knot

holding cord
knotting cord
Double half-hitch

holding cord
knotting cord

Square knot (flat)

NOTE: To make diagonal half-hitch the holding cord is held diagonally.

Half knot

piece of driftwood in illustration on left
Lark's head

group of cords tied together
cord 2 on top of loop made by cord 1
Stage 1
Stage 2
Josephine knot

STRING: Linear structures in two and three dimensions

Offcuts of string, cord, thick thread, baling cord (nylon), etc. are often discarded by factories, stores and offices. Collecting over a period of time will result in a wide assortment of useful material that can be used for linear structures in two or three dimensions. Some rods, wires and bits of board will be needed to allow an exploration of line and plane relationships.

Below, three linear structures from scrap materials including assorted strings. Test pieces by 13 year olds exploring the behaviour of lines in space.

Supports

Decide on the kind of form you wish to explore:

a Lines strung over a flat surface, e.g. for curve-stitching (thread, fine string).

b Lines strung from or across rods and bars.

c Lines strung from fixed points within two or more planes (e.g. working within an open box).

Using dowelling or metal rod supports

The base of the construction to the right of the photograph is a piece of plywood shaped to make an octagon shape. A hole drilled in the centre matches the size of available rod – in this case a piece of hollow aluminium tube. Stiff wire is fixed to the top of the tube to make four horizontal arms or eight, if preferred.

Strings are arranged horizontally on the base and between the points of the octagon and the four arms.

Using three, four or five sides of an open box

Linear ideas can also be explored within a hollow box-like form – which recalls the building-up of a model stage setting.

Use a heavy board for one side (the base) and thinner pieces for vertical sides. Fasten the sides with PVA adhesive and panel pins.

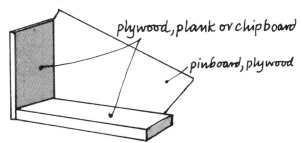

plywood, plank or chipboard

pinboard, plywood

When working out points between which to stretch the string, use regular mathematical intervals, e.g. equal spacing or the Fibonacci series (1 – 1 – 2 – 3 – 5 – 8 – 13 – 21, etc.) expressed in millimetres. Fix strings with small staples. This method achieves a form of three-dimensional curve-stitching but other arrangements can be devised.

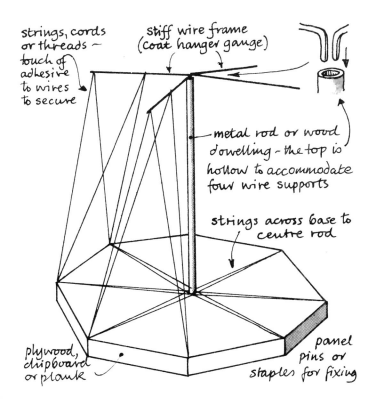

strings, cords or threads – touch of adhesive to wires to secure

stiff wire frame (coat hanger gauge)

metal rod or wood dowelling – the top is hollow to accommodate four wire supports

strings across base to centre rod

plywood, chipboard or plank

panel pins or staples for fixing

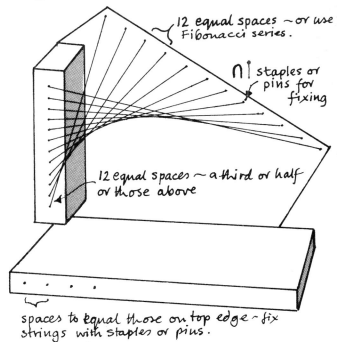

12 equal spaces ~ or use Fibonacci series.

staples or pins for fixing

12 equal spaces ~ a third or half or those above

spaces to equal those on top edge – fix strings with staples or pins.

PIANO PARTS 1

Another interesting waste material is the interior mechanism of a piano – called the piano action. Each key-to-hammer movement consists of some sixteen pieces of shaped wood (according to the type and period of the instrument) and other parts of felt and wire. Multiply this by the number of notes to a piano (about 85) and you have over 1300 individual pieces of shaped wood and many of felt and wire.

Source of supply
Obviously old piano actions are not often available, but they do have to be discarded sometimes. Try all secondhand dealers, piano restorers, house clearance firms, etc. Some restorers keep the outer casing but discard the mechanism, some repairers may throw out a few parts that are faulty. You may have to wait for some time so it is worth asking of your own relations and friends whether they know of any old pianos that would otherwise be burnt or dumped.

Preparation
Remove the individual actions from their framework. Take an action apart with pliers, screwdrivers, bradawls, etc. until you have the shapes you require. Soak in warm, soapy water for 10 to 15 minutes. This will clean all the parts and loosen the felt pads and the glued joints. Store the various shapes in separate containers.

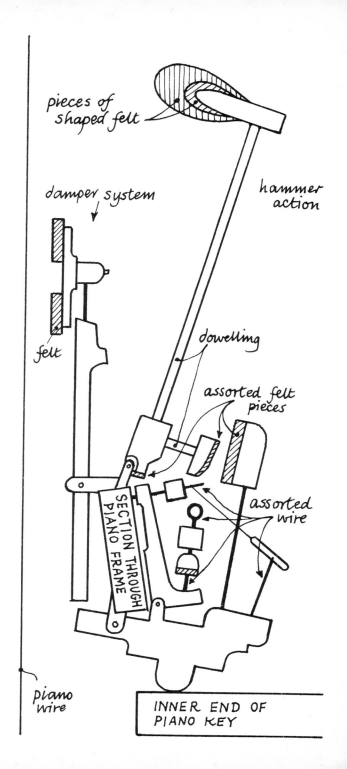

Piano action : cross-section of a typical key-to-hammer movement that is designed to hit a single piano wire. This example shows sixteen wooden pieces – many of which are used in the various craft projects illustrated on these pages. In addition, there are pieces of felt (shaded) and wire (thick black lines). See page 185 for the use of hammer felts in costume jewellery.

Small projects

The faculty of invention and the creative urge of the young child can often be stimulated by the manipulation of unusual shapes. These pre-formed piano parts will suggest some entirely new and original ways of making things provided that the projects are undertaken in an open-ended way related to principles of play and enjoyment. One example illustrated below is ideal for young fingers: a range of ships and boats from very simple units to more complex structures. The eight pieces of piano action shown in the foreground have been used in different ways to make the seven types of boat. The pieces can be glued together with any wood adhesive (PVA, Evo-Stik 'W', Bostik or Cascamite). The boats can be varnished or painted with waterproof paints (oil or gloss) and will float. For this purpose, balance by adding a few screws underneath as a keel.

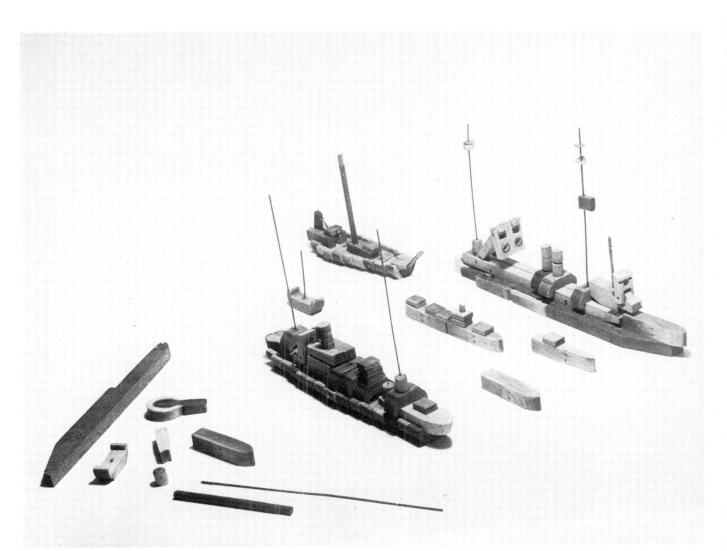

PIANO PARTS 2:
Architectural models

The older child, using a wide range of individual pieces, can construct models of building sites, urban areas, dock areas (cranes, ships and warehouses), high-rise flats and similar kinds of architectural model.

A repeating pattern of shaped wood pieces lends itself to models of this kind and often leads to quite original ideas while at the same time developing an awareness of town planning methods.

Building site
The building site shown above right incorporates both individual pieces (**A** to **E**) and some only partially dismantled (**F**).

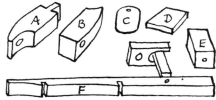

All the pieces below are incorporated in the urban area illustrated right. All pieces are glued with PVA adhesive (impact adhesive would do). Finish with clear polyurethane varnish or acrylic paint.

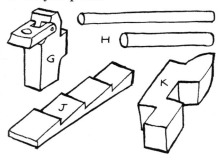

*Building site : part **F** (see drawing, left) is used to construct the flats in the left foreground and for the crane.*

Urban areas
The illustration below shows a large model that is built on a hexagonal base of scrap plywood from most of the pieces in a piano action. The flats in the background are built as for the previous model. The cranes along the river in centre are from piece **G**. The industrial area has dowel pieces (**H**) for chimneys and wedge-shaped pieces (**J**) for factory roofs. The housing in the foreground interlocks pieces (**K**) and has cylinders of wood shavings between the buildings.

3: Assemblages

If the action is kept intact many interesting spatial arrangements can be assembled. One example is illustrated below. Glue with an impact or PVA adhesive.

4: Jewellery

Necklace and collar 'jewellery' decoration can be made entirely from the felt hammer heads. A decorative collar is shown below; other arrangements could include many other pieces as well as the hammer head.

The outer layer can be soaked off (see page 182) and used as a separate shape. Pliers will be needed to remove the thick felt from the wooden head. As the felt is held by wire staples, use a pointed tool (awl or large nail) to prise it away.

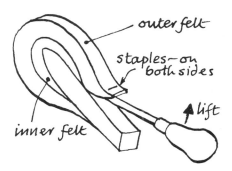

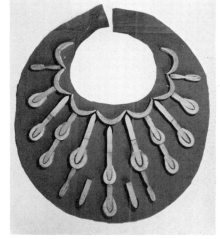

Glue parts to a felt collar.

RUBBER: Costume accessories

The inner tubes from the tyres of lorries and tractors are a very useful material for stage costumes. Tyre distributors or service stations will probably let you have one or two discarded inner tubes.

The illustration below shows characters from a production of 'Thistle in a Donkey Field' by Richard Tydman. Sub-titled 'A vegetable parable with distinct animal connections', it requires a wide range of shape, pattern and texture in the costumes to symbolise and suggest the vegetable kingdom within the context of a science fantasy. Rubber inner tubes were ideal for making collars, belts and bracelets – details are given on the opposite page. Headdresses were built on fabric or felt hats with scrap plastic, cotton reels, etc.

Ways of cutting an inner tube will depend on the size of the tube and the size of accessory needed. In the example illustrated, large collars and belts were cut along the circumference of the tube (1) while smaller collars, bracelets, etc. were cut across the section of tube (2).

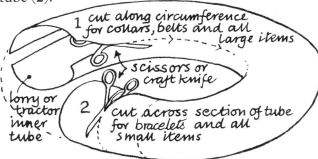

Bracelet

Cutting

Measure the wrist and allow 50 mm overlap for fixing. Decide on the width and cut two pieces of cross-section with a craft knife or scissors.

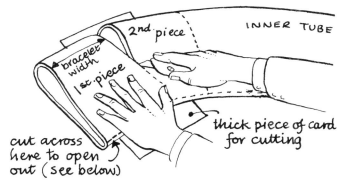

Shaping

Cut through the loop and lay the piece flat. Mark out your design and cut round it.

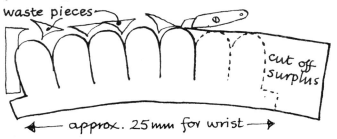

Fixing and decorating

Sew on press studs with needle, thread and thimble.

Stick on decorations with an impact adhesive. Spray with metallic paint if desired.

Large collars, crowns or belts

Cutting

Cut round the inner and outer circumferences of an inner tube (see general cutting diagram, 1). Then cut lengths from these circles to suit each actor's measurements – allowing extra for overlapping and fixing. Bear in mind the natural curve of the tube – in the case of a large collar, this will fit over the shoulders of the actor.

Shaping

Mark out your design and cut round it.

Fixing and decorating

Sew on press studs with needle, thread and thimble. More than one set will be needed for a heavy collar. See **bracelet** for note on decoration.

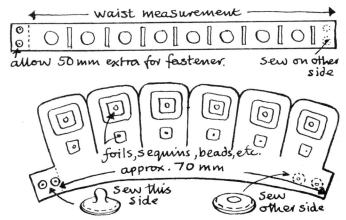

SHELLS: Collage

A vast array of shells can be found lying on many seashores. Look for variety in size if all of one kind – and for variety of colour, shape and texture if different kinds are available.

Collect limpet shells of all sizes for high relief; scallops for strong radiating lines; razor shells for bold linear shapes and patterns; periwinkles for fine detail and texture in large collages; Venus and carpet shells, cockles and cowries for bright shiny areas; shells of the edible oyster for rough texture; the common mussel for its dark blue-black colour and distinctive shape; and the auger for strong or spiky parts.

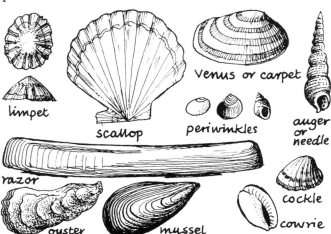

Materials

You will need a board approximately 20 mm thick that will not warp and thus cause plaster and brittle shells to crack. Marine plywoods and chipboards can be obtained as offcuts from most DIY shops and timber merchants.

Alternatively, you may occasionally find bits of old shuttering (used to form concrete walls and foundations) discarded on building sites. When cut and scraped down, these boards make strong waterproof supports.

If you want to frame your collage, use wood strip scrap from a timber yard – or buy an L-shaped moulding called 'hockey stick'.

For modelling the relief and shape of the collage use cellulose filler (Polyfilla) or any plaster that is slow to dry. (The shells will be set into this while it is still damp.)

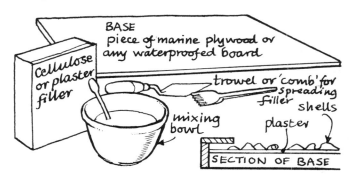

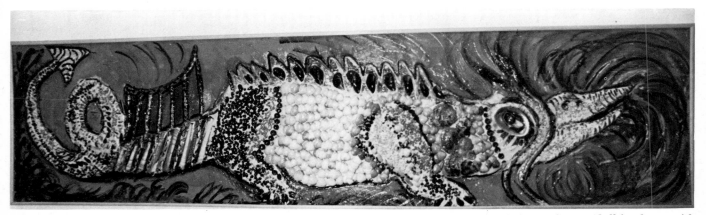

Dragon by primary school children: mussels for spine, cockles on central body, carpet shells on the neck, inverted oyster shell for the eye with mussel and acorn at the centre, razor shells on tail. A few seeds were added to the shells on the legs and tail.

Method

1 Cut a board of the required size and a piece of paper to the same size. Draw on the paper and transfer the final drawing to the board either by 'tracing' or by repeating the outlines freehand with charcoal.

2 Sort the shells into the various sizes, colours and groupings suitable to your design and arrange them tentatively on the *paper* drawing to see how they fit particular areas of the drawing. Adjust groupings and the drawing itself as necessary.

3 At this stage or before you may wish to raise parts of your design in relief. This can be done by building up layers of plaster filler or by gluing and tacking thin layers of plywood to the base and covering them with a layer of plaster. It may be necessary to repeat your drawing on the new surface.

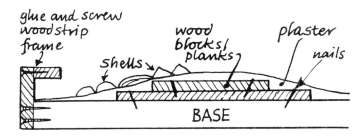

4 Select part of the design (such as the head or body of the fish) which has a well-defined outline. Dampen the board (or the relief surface) to help adhesion and to retard drying time, and then spread it with plaster filler about 3 mm thick. If the drawing fades, redraw as necessary.

5 Transfer the shells to the board from their position on the paper drawing. Press each shell lightly into the wet plaster. Experiment by laying shells down at different angles.

6 Work on a section adjacent to this first area in a similar way and continue thus over the whole surface of the board. If you can, complete the whole design before the plaster dries. This will hold the design together and prevent cracking later.

7 Make a small cone of paper and use it like a cake icing nozzle. Fill with plaster filler and squeeze gently to push out a worm of plaster for bands, borders, ridges and spots on the design. Or you can reduce the relief by gouging out channels in the still damp plaster with a smooth stick or old toothbrush handle.

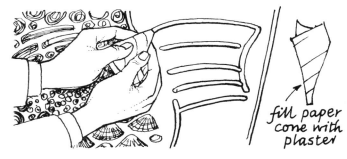

8 When the plaster is quite dry, the surface may be painted where it is not covered by shells – or left plaster-colour. Painted or plain, the surface can be textured.

9 When completely dry, the collage can be brushed over with clear varnish. Use gloss, semi-gloss or matt as preferred.

10 Finally – if you wish – tack or screw a frame or edging round the board. Suspend on the wall as you would any picture, either on a hook by a cord (fixed to the back of the collage by screw eyes) or secured direct to a wall with screws and Rawlplugs (where tops of screws show, fill in with plaster).

Part of the dragon collage opposite, showing detail of shells.

CANE

Cane offcuts can be obtained from anyone engaged in basketry work and make a useful scrap item for linear structures. The example on the right shows work by a 14 year old from a class project for which the starting point was the idea of flowing lines within a three-dimensional design.

The large decorated fabric collar below shows a combination of cane pieces with oddments from a piano hammer (including the hammer felt). If the cane offcuts are long enough, they can be soaked in water and formed into spirals, zig-zags and other patterns. Glue with an impact adhesive and sew onto collar with strong thread. Paint in metallic colours.

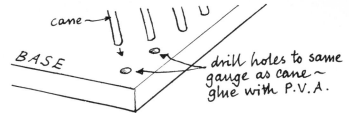

cane

BASE

drill holes to same gauge as cane ~ glue with P.V.A.

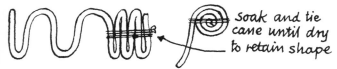

soak and tie cane until dry to retain shape

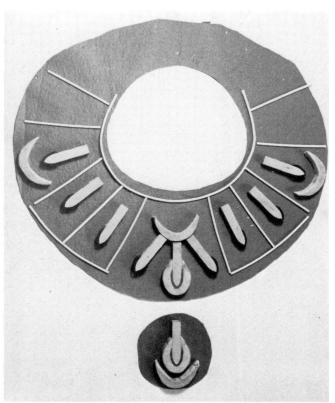

Above: a cane structure by a 14 year old using cane offcuts on a three-wall support. A piece of Meccano near the base has determined the spacing for each piece of cane.

Left: decorated collar with a felt base decorated with cane pieces and parts of a piano hammer.

ODDS AND ENDS:
Collage pictures

Practically any small object can be used to make a collage: nails, bits of broken china, wire, matchsticks, shells (see pages 188–9), lentils, pasta, string, acorns, various hard berries, pine needles, etc.

The two examples on this page show a wide use of scrap oddments. The method of application is as for the previous two pages. An alternative technique for fixing is to glue each item with a strong impact adhesive (Evo-Stik, Bostik) and to fill the spaces with plaster of a creamy consistency. Wipe away the surplus when it has dried. (This technique is less successful for a bright, clean finish on small detailed items, but quite suitable for pieces of ceramic tile or broken china.)

Right: owl collage. Eyes are buttons surrounded by blue tacks, cocktail and toothpick sticks. The wing is of winged sycamore seeds, the chest of pasta and Rawlplugs, the feet of matchsticks, and the berries on the branches of beads.

Below: fish. The head is built up from plaster with an eye of periwinkle set within an inverted limpet shell. The hanging under the mouth is of straw and beads; the fins are of bits of red celluloid decorated with Polyfilla piping; the lower body is of large sequins and 'coke' bottle tops; the tail of a large scallop shell with Polyfilla piping; the upper body is studded with acorns.

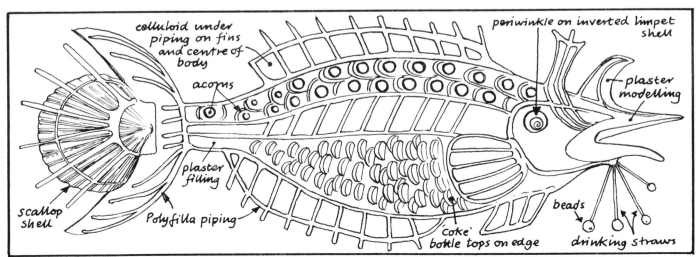

celluloid under piping on fins and centre of body

periwinkle on inverted limpet shell

acorns

plaster modelling

plaster filling

scallop shell

Polyfilla piping

'coke' bottle tops on edge

beads

drinking straws

DUST, POWDER, GRAINS, etc.

Sawdust, wood chippings, sand, old plaster, vermiculite grains and other small packing granules in plastic materials can all be used for a variety of surface treatment. The finer grains are most suitable for texturing the ground surfaces of scale models. Coarser grains can be used in mask-making to create unusual textures for monsters and fantastic creatures. Even larger grains can be useful for theatre work where they make interesting wall surfaces in conjunction with skilfully oblique stage lighting.

All grains should be sprinkled onto a freshly glued surface. Blow the surplus off the wet glue and leave the rest to set. Paint can be applied when the textured surface is thoroughly dry.

Fine grains : sawdust (or sand)

Finger patterns in wet plaster

Part of an octopus costume for a play with an underwater plot – surface uses vermiculite granules. The head and tentacles are made from the inner tube of a lorry tyre (see page 186).

Old plaster made up and spread; roughened with various tools whilst wet

Chippings and shavings

Collages

Sands and grains of different colours can be used to make collage pictures – with areas of different textures.

All this fine debris can be saved from DIY jobs of various kinds.

BOOK LIST

These books are generally available for reference in libraries even though some may be out of print.

Collage
Practice of Collage, by Brian French and Anne Butler *Mills & Boon*

Introducing Paper Collage, by Robin Capon *Batsford*

Corrugated cardboard
Corrugated Carton Crafting, by Dick van Voorst, in Little Craft Books series *Oak Tree Press* (*Sterling* in U.S.A.)

Dolls
Doll Making for Everyone, by Helen Young *Yoseloff*

Doll Making: a creative approach, by Jean Ray Laury *Van Nostrand Reinhold*

Dolls. Traditional and Topical, by Benbow, Dunlop and Luckin *Harrap*

Embroidery
Introducing Design in Embroidery, by Betty Chicken *Batsford*

Fabric techniques
Tie and Dye, leaflet from *Dylon International*

Patchwork, by Averil Colby *Batsford*

Fabrics and Threads for Schools, by Anne Coleman *Batsford*

Tie-and-Dye as a Present Day Craft, by Anne Maile *Mills & Boon*

Macramé
Technique of Macramé, by Bonny Schmid-Burleson *Batsford*

Masks
How to Make Masks, by M. K. Skinner *Studio Vista*

Cut and Colour Paper Masks, by Michael Grater *Dover*

Metal
Take a Tin Can: How to Make Decorative Models, by Richard Slade *Faber*

Ideas for Jewellery, by Ian Davidson *Batsford*

Simple Wire Sculpture, by Elizabeth Gallop *Studio Vista*

Metal and Wire Sculpture, by Gruber *Oak Tree Press*

Creating with Metal, by Granstrom *Van Nostrand Reinhold*

Mobiles
Making Mobiles, by Anne and Christopher Morey *Studio Vista*

Model making
First Models in Cardboard, by G. Roland Smith *Dryad*

Paper and card
Creative Paper Crafts, by Ernst Röttger *Batsford*

Art and Design in Papier-Mâché, by Karen Knykendall *Kaye & Ward*

One Piece of Card, by George Aspden *Batsford*

Plastics
Craftwork in Plastic, in Leisure Craft series *Search Press*

Designing with Plastics, Schools Council Design and Craft Education Project *Edward Arnold*

Creative Plastics, by David Rees *Studio Vista*

Sculpture
Practical Sculpture, by Robert Dawson *Studio Vista*

Starting with Sculpture, by Robert Dawson *Studio Vista*

Stage costume and properties
Stage Costumes and How to Make Them, by Julia Tompkins *Pitman*

Stage Crafts, by Chris Hoggett *Black*

Wood crafts

Foundation of Design in Wood, by F. O. Zanker *Dryad*

Wooden Images, by Norman Laliberte and M. Jones *Van Nostrand Reinhold*

Plywood, by Rolf Hartung *Batsford*

Woodcarving for Beginners, by Charles Graveney *Studio Vista*

Creative Wood Craft, by Ernst Röttger *Batsford*

General crafts

The Book of Crafts, edited by Henry Pluckrose *Evans*

The Family Book of Things to Make and Do *Reader's Digest*

Art from Scrap Materials, by Robin Capon *Batsford*

Popular Crafts, in the Golden Hands series *Marshall Cavendish*

INDEX

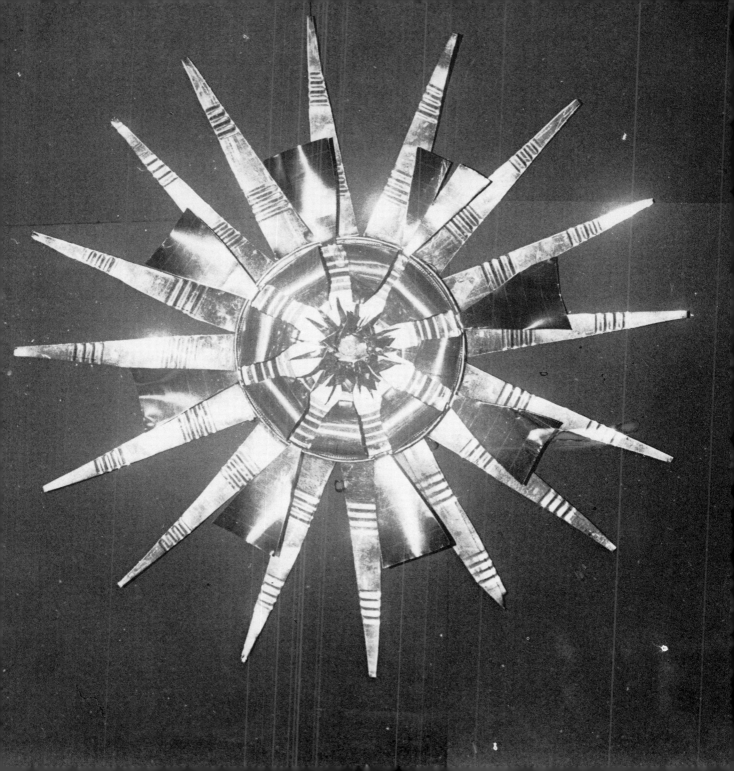